Hans Coper

Tony Birks

HANS COPER

Icon Editions

1817

HARPER & ROW, PUBLISHERS, New York

Cambridge, Philadelphia, San Francisco,

London, Mexico City, São Paulo, Sydney

HANS COPER. Copyright © 1983 by Tony Birks.
All rights reserved. Printed in Great Britain. No part
of this book may be used or reproduced in any
manner whatsoever without written permission
except in the case of brief quotations embodied in
critical articles and reviews. For information address
Harper & Row, Publishers, Inc., 10 East 53rd Street,
New York, N.Y. 10022. Published simultaneously in
Canada by Fitzhenry & Whiteside Limited, Toronto.

FIRST U.S. EDITION
ISBN: 0-06-430390-X

LIBRARY OF CONGRESS CATALOG CARD NUMBER: 83-49060

84 85 86 87 88 10 9 8 7 6 5 4 3 2 1

Contents

Part of the Hans Coper Memorial Collection at the Sainsbury Centre for Visual Arts, displayed in the context of new acquisitions, February 1983.

1 Introduction

Pottery is a very tactile medium. It makes a difference to one's appreciation of a pot if one holds it in the hand. Like sculpture, it has to be experienced in the round, but generally pottery is small enough to be taken up and felt, the fingers reinforcing the eyes with their sensitivity to texture and form. The experience of holding a Hans Coper pot is an unusual one, and it helps to bring home both the complexity of the inter-related shapes and the simplicity and purity towards which Hans always aimed. He referred to his pots, with affection, as 'these odd things I make', and had a genuine humility regarding all his work. He was determined that it should remain pottery, not sculpture, by ensuring that everything he produced was a container – whether for fruit, flowers, coffee or candles – and by submitting always to the discipline of the wheel as his starting point for the development of the shape.

But of course his pots are much more than containers, for they are the end product of a double process of refinement: by the intellect, which ensured a careful harmonic purity from the constant reworking of the relationships between forms, and by the technique, in which precision and sensitivity produced a result which has, in place of spontaneity, a curious combination of tranquillity and tension. In addition, there is something else: although his pots, like music, are abstract, they have the same inexplicable ability to arouse emotion.

Though he called himself a potter, and sometimes a ceramist, pronounced classically with a hard 'c', he allied himself not with other potters of his own kind but with two groups of makers. Firstly, with the anonymous potters of the distant past and of tribal cultures, whose artefacts were refined by endless repetition and who saw no separation between form and decoration; secondly with certain twentieth century artists whose work is the result of a compulsion to get closer and closer to a basic truth. In Hans's own words, '. . . like a demented piano tuner one is trying to approximate a phantom pitch.' I am thinking in particular of Giacometti and Brancusi who shared in their lives so many precepts with Hans. They were ex-patriates who left their native country and settled in a foster country where their art flourished. Such artists are, of course, very numerous but the creative people Hans admired most came into this category: not only Brancusi and Giacometti but Beckett, Stravinsky and Chagall. And Hans himself settled firmly in Britain, away from the Germany of his birth. I am sure that this transplantation had an effect on his work. He had no connection with English ceramics, nor any regional or national style. Within Britain, where he made such an impact on pottery from 1950 onwards, he is inevitably regarded as a European, but in fact he owed no allegiances. He is a truly original figure.

He broke new ground with the shapes he made in fired clay, and in form, colour, surface and texture he created his own visual vocabulary. But it is not the outward manifestation of his technique alone which counts. If he influences others, it is in directing the modern potter towards a concept in pottery which is ancient in origin, but new in our time: fusing the functional with the cultural and symbolic. The photograph on page 6 of part of the Memorial Collection in the Sainsbury Centre at the University of East Anglia in Norwich shows how comfortably his modern work lies alongside the artefacts of the ancient past.

The illustrations in this book are designed to show as wide a spectrum as possible of Hans's pots and other creative work in clay. They can only go part way, however, in illuminating his character, his influence on others, and his life. Hans Coper had an ability to teach with patience and with insight, and profound sympathy for all individual human beings. Not only potters and architects, but builders and teachers, men and women from all walks of life experienced his exceptional charisma. He was no ordinary person. Those closest to him were always aware of his abundance of humour and his delight in the absurdities of life. His was the wit of the outsider, the non-joiner. Next to his work, people, not theories, were what mattered most, and the many friends who helped me with research especially into the early years before I knew Hans, have remarked on the value he placed on humility, and his scepticism for officialdom and any form of self-importance in others. One long-standing friend, Reg Mutter, wrote to me: *'He had X-ray eyes when it came to pretension; he perceived the nakedness of Emperors.'*

2
Germany, London, Canada & the Pioneer Corps

Hans Coper was born on April 8th, 1920, in Chemnitz, a few miles from the Czechoslovakian border. His father, Julius, was Jewish, though his mother, Erna, was not. The Copers already had one son, Walter, who was five years old when Hans was born, and all through Hans's childhood the family lived in Reichenbach, a small town near Chemnitz. The German tradition, maintained to the present time, of sending a little boy off to school on his first day carrying an enormous cone full of sweets is illustrated by this photograph of Hans at the age of six, with a 'schuletute' almost as big as himself. A prosperous middle-class background is indicated by the clothes, though the child's expression suggests a sad acceptance of rather than a delight in these trappings.

Hans's father was the manager of a small textile mill and must have been a competent and successful businessman. Stability in Germany there was not, in the 1920s, but for the Coper family at least there was prosperity. Hans's own early memories include a chauffeur-driven automobile, with cut-glass decanters and drinks for the passengers in the back. There is another memory of his childhood treasured by Hans for its surrealism: Hans's father's textile mill employed women weavers in a hot room. To keep cool the women weavers stripped to the waist (something unthinkable in Britain in between the wars, but remember that Chemnitz was next door to Bohemia). Stripping-off, however, was not enough and the women got hotter and hotter with the efforts of their work, and white fluff from the cotton would stick to their bodies. Hans – he must have been very young at the time for he was looking up through the warps of the great looms – saw the girl weavers like great furry teddybears covered in fluff. It would be interesting to know if this was a single clandestine visit which impressed him so, or if his childish figure was often seen in the textile works.

2 May 1926

September sunshine in the Coper's garden in Reichenbach. Hans, aged 8, is in the foreground, his father and cousin sit in the wicker chairs.

The Copers' home in Reichenbach had a large garden, where the photograph above was taken. In a letter to her sister, Hans's mother describes this picture as 'a Sunday idyll in the Coper garden'. Hans, aged eight, is in the foreground. His father, gently smiling, sits in the wicker chair in the sunshine. Hans was a happy, popular boy, though rather solitary – exactly the sort of contradiction which stayed with him all through his life. His passions were his Meccano set and motor cars, and he would spend hours alone in the family attic, building models or drawing cars and motorcycles. By the time he was twelve his family was aware of his talent as a draughtsman, and his skill in painting and the crafts, but the times were changing and the pleasant years had come to an end. As Hans entered adolescence in 1933, Adolf Hitler became Reichs Chancellor, and the Storm Troopers who had sprung up out of the political disarray of the 1920s now had official status. In 1933, too, the Gestapo was formed, the concentration camp in Dachau was opened, and the harassment of Jewish businessmen had begun in earnest, with a boycotting of Jewish firms on April 1st of that year. Hans's father Julius was most probably held in local respect by Jew and non-Jew alike, but he must have come under increasing pressure, and he either lost his job or resigned from the textile mill in Reichenbach. The family moved to Dresden, where they lived in an imposing house – No. 6 Walderseeplatz (shown right) – an unusual residence, bizarre by British standards and, though modern, quite typical of the individuality which made Dresden such a striking Baroque city.

No. 6 Walderseeplatz, Dresden.

10

The next two years must have been a harsh contradiction of the soft years of childhood. At school in Dresden Hans found his examination results and his school reports 'doctored' by the National Socialist teachers, so that his report would denigrate him in the eyes of the school and his fellows, and by distressing his family, nicely spoil Christmas, Easter and the start of any holiday.

By 1935 the family had moved again, this time to a flat in Leipzig. They were on the run now, and the two boys could not continue studying, nor could they get a job. Using what influence he could by calling on his previous status in the textile business, Hans's father managed to organise an apprenticeship for his younger son in a spinning mill, but in the words of his brother Walter, 'Hans did not like it, and it did not last long.' It seems likely that Hans could have taken to the technical training readily enough, and I must suppose that it was either the effects of his Jewishness or the need to keep his Jewish status a secret which made him an unwilling apprentice. In any event, he lost his job, just as his father had done two years before, and for Julius Coper the attentions of the Nazis were making life more and more unpleasant. It is hard to imagine how suicide could ever have been undertaken for the benefit of the family; yet these were the years when many Jewish heads of families took their own lives to improve the lot of their wives and children, especially where the wife was not Jewish. It is in this context that we must consider Herr Coper's suicide in June 1936, although the circumstances are not known. Hans was barely sixteen, his brother twenty-one. The family of three moved back to Dresden, and the following year Hans's brother Walter left Germany. There was a Coper uncle in Argentina, and a job was organised for Walter in a textile mill in South America. Hans and his mother travelled to Hamburg to see Walter on to the boat, and then went back to Dresden. Erna Coper thought her 'little boy' was too young to emigrate, and should at least learn a trade. The reality of the future had come home to mother and son, and survival depended, it seemed, on being able to do a useful job. Hans managed to enrol for training in textile engineering at a technical school in Dresden and studied there until he, too, packed his suitcase for emigration in early 1939. Mrs Erna Coper was non-Jewish and presumably had less to fear than her sons, so she stayed put in Dresden. Hans left behind a bourgeois life that had been broken apart. He left behind a beloved motor bicycle, his friends and all his youthful activities, and quit the amazing city of Dresden.

As far as can be established Hans was not involved in any political activity, but being Jewish – or half-Jewish – was dangerous enough, and the route to sanctuary must have been traumatic. He had arranged a sponsor in England, a Mr H. Kahn who had emigrated in the 1930s and may well have been a business associate of Hans's late father; he was certainly not a relative. To get to England in safety, Hans had the help of the Quakers – The Society of Friends – in England. He spent six months in 1939 hiding in a hotel in Wiesbaden, where there were family connections, waiting for a 'safe' train out of Germany. By then any traveller with a Jewish name was likely to be detained by the Gestapo, and when Hans's train was stopped and searched he hid his papers under the seat and climbed out of a window while the searchers went past, just managing to scramble back on board as the train moved off.

He arrived in London in 1939 with a portmanteau and very little money. In the portmanteau was a dress suit, and if Hans had thought that this would be 'de rigueur' in the England he had never before visited, it was an idea he soon abandoned, and he took the suit to a pawn shop. He had spent hours and hours in Germany listening to the transmissions of the BBC, and through the radio and films he became fascinated by England, and its football teams with strange names like Aston Villa, and longed to be able to visit the country. In the event, he found he had built up a rather inaccurate picture. He received a coolish welcome from the Kahn family in Hampstead Garden Suburb, though the German housekeeper Annie warmed to the thin and startled-looking boy who, she said, was always hungry. There was no room for him in the Kahns' house, or at least none was offered, and so Hans took digs in Gower Street, Bloomsbury, near the Slade School and opposite the Royal Academy of Dramatic Art. He had left Germany just in time. On September 3rd war was declared and so Hans, the refugee, was officially an enemy alien.

It is not clear whether Hans could speak English when he arrived. He must have learned some English at school, but in his lodgings in Gower Street he found himself among drama students from RADA, and it was from them that he learned the language. He would listen to the embryo actors learning and speaking their parts, he himself holding the book and acting as a prompt. It was an unusual and remarkably effective way of learning the King's English. His pronunciation was faultless and accentless. Considering what a great deal of time he later spent in England among refugees with strong German, Viennese or Russian accents, it is quite astonishing (though much in keeping with the man) that no one could find the slightest trace of accent in his adopted tongue. German friends would speak of his Saxony accent in German, though Hans spoke less and less in his native language, and would only use German words with other Germans when at a loss for the precise English equivalent.

It is known that the first few months in England were for Hans a period of great depression. We cannot be sure now what he was thinking at the time, but the escape from the Nazis certainly left a permanent emotional distaste for Germany as a whole which would have been out of character in a man so free of prejudice if he had done anything but keep it strictly to himself.

This book is about a potter, not about politics. To dwell on his teenage years in Dresden under the persecution would be inappropriate and in any event the facts are not known. That Hans never spoke of his personal experiences to anyone is eloquent enough. His childhood security had been rapidly eroded away. The three years between his father's suicide and his arrival in England were his seventeenth, eighteenth and nineteenth years, a time in most people's lives that is clearly remembered and cherished. Hans reached England with almost no possessions, and almost no friends, and to his many friends in later years he never said more than that 'those years were terrible'.

He had a little money coming to him by way of the Quakers in London, organised by his brother Walter from South America, but this was scarcely enough to provide him with food and lodging. He had nothing to do, his technical studies were interrupted, and he tried to end his life in London by gassing himself. He had not got enough money for the gas meter – a fact he recalled in later years with much amusement, though clearly life was not funny for him at the time. That he should have made such an attempt indicates how Hans's fortune and spirit had declined in this short period of years. Shortly afterwards, in any event, Hans was caught up in the wave of internment which all refugees from National Socialism had to face in early 1940. First of all he was called to a tribunal, operated by hurriedly appointed officials who took it upon themselves to assess the danger to national security posed by each individual refugee. Categories were A,

B and C. 'A' category candidates were those who were thought to be spies or agents of subversion, and were immediately interned. Categories 'B' and 'C' were left with their freedom for a time. Hans was category 'B'. With the national crisis deepening and invasion threatened, in the Spring of 1940 all 'B' and 'C' category alien males were put behind barbed wire in the process described in Peter and Leni Gillman's recent book, aptly called *Collar the Lot*.

After the trauma of getting away from persecution, it must have been with a great sense of betrayal that many Germans, as well as Italians, Austrians and Russians packed a suitcase again and found themselves confined and in as promiscuous a mix as they had ever experienced in their lives. Hans was arrested on May 12th, 1940, and sent to an internment camp in Huyton, in Lancashire. I imagine that he took his few personal possessions with him. The camp was a half-built housing estate intended for workers in Liverpool; it was quickly surrounded with barbed wire by the Home Office, and a great deal of straw was provided. By filling sacks with this straw the men made their own bedding, but there was absolutely no furniture in the half-finished houses, and twelve men were allocated to each house. The living conditions in the camp were much criticised – no newspapers, no radios, no towels – but for Hans and his fellows worse was yet to come, and Hans was by now learning to develop the fatalism and quiet acceptance of his circumstances which characterised his later life. After six weeks in this camp he was embarked on a troop-carrying ship called the *Ettrick*, bound for another internment camp in Canada.

In talking to German and Russian refugees who were interned with Hans, or interned at the same time, I have been surprised by how little bitterness they seem to have felt, both in retrospect and even at the time. With a tradition, at least in earlier centuries, of being hospitable to refugees, Mother England would have been showing an unexpectedly distrustful face to the very people who had already suffered at the hands of Nazism. But it was worse than that, as some internees were clearly shown more favour than others, and many refugees were in a state of great distress. The youthful Hans seems to have regained his equilibrium so completely that he was able to offer mature advice and a helping hand to others whilst at Huyton. Indeed, although Hans retained no friends at all from his Chemnitz, Dresden and Leipzig years, internment produced warm friendships which continued for the rest of his life. It was, for example, in the internment camp at

Internees at the Huyton Camp, making their own mattresses.

Huyton that he met Joseph (Jupp) Dernbach from the Rheinland, who remained one of Hans's best friends and appears again in later chapters. Billeted in neighbouring houses, they played chess together and talked, and Jupp, who was ten years older than Hans, was impressed by the young man's modern outlook and intellect. The contact was temporarily broken when Hans was one of those put on the *Ettrick*, which sailed for the St Lawrence on July 3rd, 1940.

On the same day news came that another ship, the *Arandora Star*, which had left only two days beforehand, had been torpedoed by a U-boat off Ireland, with the loss of 800 lives. Many of the survivors came back to Liverpool, but not until Hans's ship had left, carrying over 2,500 men. This was more than twice the number she was built for, and the journey was frightening and long. On board were Germans, Austrians and Italians, including 900 prisoners of war. The commander of the soldiers detailed to supervise the deportees wrote, 'Far too many prisoners and aliens for quarters available.' Perhaps distinctions got blurred, and maybe Hans was particularly unfortunate, but he suffered persecution and even anti-Semitism on the voyage, and many others on that ship recalled bitterly that the prisoners of war received better treatment than the refugees from Nazi Germany. In any event, he crossed the Atlantic in the forward hold *with the hatches battened down*. This meant, of course, that in the likely event of a torpedo attack such as had destroyed the sister ship only a few days earlier, the Jews and refugees heaped together in the hold would have had no escape from drowning. For a youthful and healthy middle-class German boy from Dresden, this was the low point in terms of loss of human dignity. He could hardly have been prepared for the squalor and degradation of the *Ettrick*.

The voyage ended in Quebec on July 13th, and Hans was sent to 'Camp N' at Sherbrooke, a French-Canadian town near the United States border, where the State of Maine joins Vermont. The camp consisted of two railway sheds, each containing about 200 men, surrounded by barbed wire and watch towers. The guards and soldiers removed and kept all personal valuables, and although there were beds and latrines the impression the camp gave was that of a place of punishment. The internees formed themselves into small social groups, and a surviving member of Hans's own group has described to me the experience Hans must have shared with them. The initial shock was that the Canadians saw no distinction between the internees and prisoners of war. They had been told by the Home Office in Britain to expect prisoners and subversives, and this was what the camps were prepared for: lines of mattresses or boards, naked bulbs, no partitions for privacy, and in later months a fearfully cold winter outside. This was, as far as the inmates could tell, not just a temporary stage: it was home.

The first action of the internees was to go on hunger strike. Rumours in the camp were naturally abundant, and some of the time the news was good. Conditions improved as American financial aid arrived in the camp, and especially when radios were made available. Morale was raised enormously when a Home Office official, Alexander Patterson, came over in November 1940, officially to put the records straight about the status of the men as internees, not prisoners. The worst, in terms of humiliation, was behind them. It is interesting that Hans's friends in the camp were able to find in this young man a source of comfort, one who described the future as full of hope and the present as a great deal better than it might have been in Germany.

Somehow in the railway sheds of Sherbrooke the talents and skills that are always recounted in stories of incarceration started to appear. A printing press was made operational: improvisation helped by artists and engineers. No doubt someone made a chess set, and Hans would have played, but not with Jupp Dernbach, for they had lost touch with each other after the Huyton camp in England. Hans is remembered, however, for having sat on his bunk doing hundreds of drawings of his colleagues. Here in Sherbrooke he met Fritz Wolf, an artist from Breslau who became to him a sort of mentor. It was Fritz, not the Bauhaus example of his native Saxony, who introduced Hans to the world of modern art, and it was in Canada that Hans decided that he wanted to become a sculptor.

There was constant fear in the camp that the Germans would invade Britain, and the French-Canadians would for some reason turn on the inmates and send them back to Germany. However, Patterson interviewed the internees one by one, and arranged for some to return to England. Freeing the internees in Canada or arranging for them to transfer to the United States was difficult, but those able-bodied men who were prepared to join the Pioneer Corps of the British Army were sent back in batches. This meant returning right into the jaws of war, but as an alternative to Canadian internment it appealed to many. Perhaps some

wanted to show their captors where in the European conflict their true loyalties lay. Hans was amongst those who volunteered, and back he went across the Atlantic. The date was June 1941. Before he left he gave to a fellow internee, Fred Cohn, a curiously touching photograph which could not have been taken in Canada. It shows Hans in a pleasure boat, almost certainly on London's own Serpentine, pipe in mouth. His companion may have been one of the Royal Academy of Dramatic Art students.

The Pioneer Corps has been described by many emigré writers from Peter Ustinov to George Mikes. It is nowhere better described than by Victor Ross in his book *Basic British*. Victor Ross shared Hans's experiences in Canada, and like Hans was one of the 3000 deportees whose return to Britain was conditional on joining the Pioneer Corps. The hopes of building bridges and being a path-finder were soon dashed by the reality of being a Pioneer. Victor Ross writes:

> Once again I had not reckoned with the English passion for giving a thing an utterly misleading name. . . . The ground we broke was Scottish virgin soil, and our implements were picks and shovels. This was as near as we got to the true pioneering spirit: no building of bridges for us, although we played a fair amount of bridge; no sabotaging of railways, except perhaps by travelling without a warrant. Most of our time was spent under canvas, building hutted camps. As soon as one camp was ready it was occupied by ATS or Americans, while we moved to another lot of tents and started digging all over again. . . .
>
> Entertainments devised for after-duty hours were petrol drill and fire drill. Petrol drill was designed for the unlikely event that the country's entire transport system might break down and petrol would have to be manhandled across the length and breadth of the United Kingdom by a small body of Continental refugees. For this purpose we practised with five-gallon petrol tins, prised open at one end and filled to the required weight with sand. That meant that they were about one-third full, with the sand slopping about inside. It had the odd effect of making them twitch and jump like living things as they were passed along the line. Sometimes you got hold of the heavy end, which nearly knocked you over, sometimes of the empty end which meant that the weight hit you like a delayed-action bomb as the sand shifted its position.

Hans's delight in the absurd, a characteristic familiar to those who knew him in later life, had plenty of opportunity for indulgence in the Pioneer Corps. Physicists and architects, Egyptologists and circus clowns would work together with cement and trowel, laying the foundations for Nissen huts, and speaking mainly German to one another. Not all the members of the Pioneer Corps were aliens. Each detachment had, in the early days at least, an English commander, and there were English private soldiers of a rather basic sort. The English Pioneers were allowed to carry arms; the aliens were not. It was thus that an important army store near Newbury racecourse was guarded by Hans's detachment armed only with pick-axe handles.

On their return from Canada, direct to the Isle of Man, Hans and his friend Fritz Wolf had enlisted in the 93rd Company of the Pioneer Corps at Douglas, on Bastille Day in 1941, and were soon sent for training at Codford on Salisbury Plain. There were four detachments, and in the fourth detachment Hans and Fritz Wolf started on a peregrination around the south-west of England, full of comic incident but also frustrating, mindless and depressing, sometimes without any relief. The strange contradictions which were to occur through Hans's life are evident here. The Pioneer Corps drained Hans's energy, spirits and health, yet again he made vital and lasting friendships, and though subject to the constraints of army life he was, in one sense, a free man, earning a tiny pay packet and with occasional leave to travel about, free weekends and a railway warrant.

In Cirencester, Gloucestershire, he met again Jupp Dernbach, last seen at Huyton and now also a Pioneer, whose German opera-singer wife was entertaining the troops. At Ivybridge he made friends with Arthur Ross, a Danziger who shared his interests and humour. In Somerset he met Frances, later Francesca, the daughter of an English seaman, in time to become a central figure in his life and the mother of his children.

Teams of Pioneers spent months digging the trench for a pipeline which seemed to snake its way across the entire southern half of England. Hans spent six weeks at Salcombe, at the southern tip of Devon, helping to dig a deep trench for this pipeline. Jupp Dernbach volunteered for extra heavy digging here, and got a supplement to his wages, but this inducement was not enough for Hans to dig deeper and longer. Instead of swelling his wages, Hans made the most of his time off. He remembered his six weeks in Salcombe with intense pleasure, for here, in the dark days of 1942, he learned to ride. With Fritz Wolf he would ride on the deserted sandy beaches of South Devon, and into the sea. They both remembered vividly the young English girl who would ride with them, little more than a child, and very beautiful. The coastline around Salcombe has a pre-Cambrian beauty unlike anything Hans would have seen in Germany, and he recalled this period as the only island of pleasure in the year of manual work which took him on a slow

From the left: Pioneers Wolf, Coper, Ross, Friedenheim, Schliemer and Swarsenski in their billet at Candle Court, Milborne Port, Sherborne.

progression eastwards. Hans later said that he had 'dug his way from Devon to Dover', though in fact he did not get so far.

One of the stopping points was near Weymouth, which was being bombed by the Germans. Here Hans and Fritz Wolf took leave to be the witnesses at the Yeovil wedding of Andreas Zobel, another German from Dresden in the Pioneer Corps, to Francesca, the girl from Watchet in Somerset who was now in the Land Army. Hans bought flowers for the occasion, and the quartet managed a wedding lunch at the hotel by Yeovil Station. Another Pioneer encampment was at Milborne Port near Sherborne, where the photograph above was taken in September 1942. All the Pioneers in the picture have German or Polish names, and all are smiling except for Hans, second from the left. On the extreme left is Fritz Wolf, who by now had become the major influence on Hans and a firm, if sarcastic and sardonic, friend. Fritz was not popular in the detachment, being insensitive and cruel in his humour, but Hans responded to his biting irony and certainly benefited from Fritz's understanding of modern art, sculpture and architecture. He was a trained artist of some talent, and amongst several portraits of Pioneers which have survived, there is a watercolour, shown right, of Hans now aged twenty-two in his fatigues uniform.

Whilst Fritz Wolf was always kicking against authority Hans was milder and more resigned. The days spent up to the knees in water-filled ditches, however, were taking a toll of his health. He had rheumatism

Hans in uniform. Watercolour by Fritz Wolf.

16

and back trouble, and by the time the detachment had worked its way to Hampshire Hans was put into hospital with a total breakdown. Fritz Wolf changed his name to Howard Mason, to enable him to take up active service in France (German-sounding names were not used by British soldiers on the Front Line), and for a time the friends were parted.

Hans was discharged from hospital in Southampton and from the Pioneer Corps on his twenty-third birthday, for 'ceasing to fulfil army physical requirements', though his army conduct was described as 'good'. To make a further contribution to the war effort, however, he was now sent to work on a farm in Devon. The second half of 1943 is the least well documented period of Hans's life in England. It must have been one of the most miserable. Clearly the Devon farmer had little time for Germans, and Hans had nowhere better to sleep than in the stable, sharing this bedroom not with a horse but with a hearse. The summer of 1943 was wet, and for the second time since he had touched English soil his bedding was straw. His health suffered from the physical strain and damp conditions, and pains in his back and limbs, diagnosed at the time as 'rheumatism' was in fact ankylosing spondylitis, a progressive fusion of the vertebrae which causes a stiffening of the posture and much pain.

Hans managed, however, to keep in touch with the friends he had made in the army, and got away from the farm to a rented room in London later in 1943. Very soon – incongruously quickly it might seem in this narrative – he was married to an English girl, Penelope, who had befriended him in London and nursed him back to health. But the union was short-lived, and was more for the benefit of the offspring, a baby girl called Ingrid, than for either of her parents. Hans went to Leeds, where the beautiful Francesca, last seen at her Yeovil marriage, was now living, separated from her husband, and in Spring 1944 began a long and important relationship between them. Hans explained to her that he had been 'taken by a wife', but it was in Francesca that he found a warm and loving companion, and the opportunity at last to practise his ambition to be an artist and a sculptor, with Francesca as his model. Two pounds ten shillings a week was all the couple had to live on when they came to London. They lived first in Eton Avenue near Swiss Cottage, and then in Gloucester Avenue, Camden Town, where Hans had a job first as a fireman, and then as a porter with the ABC Bakeries shifting bags of flour. Without a work permit employment was difficult, and whatever jobs Hans got did not last for long. He was a good natural mechanic – as a boy he had followed motor racing enthusiastically, and had made a hero of the legendary racer Nuvolari – and so he got work in a garage, but it was a precarious existence, cemented by nightlong sessions painting and drawing. Almost nothing remains of this work. Most of Hans's paintings were oil on paper, since canvas was too expensive, and there is only one extant canvas, a self-portrait. Francesca remembers how much of the work was discarded angrily – screwed-up balls of paper flew into the corners of the room. Hans had no teacher: he did not need one as he knew exactly what he was trying to achieve. His only artistic advisor was Fritz Wolf, now Howard Mason, who visited the couple in Gloucester Avenue en route to North Africa, where he was to become a Tank Commander in the British Army.

Francesca did her best to make a home in the tiny flat in Gloucester Avenue, though most of the furniture was orange boxes, and a visit from Hans's wife Penelope, who needed financial support, left the couple miserable at the bareness of their life. Francesca, however, understood Hans's need for time to do his own creative work, and valued his creative efforts at a time when no one else did.

Hans's daughter, Anya, was born to Francesca in December 1944, and the couple moved to a small flat in Stoke Newington. Hans got both a work permit and a job in a Kilburn factory winding armatures for electric motors, but his health was poor and hepatitis and then tuberculosis were the next things to come to plague him. The healthy and sturdy youth photographed on the Serpentine in 1939 had become very careworn, thin and enfeebled through the course of the war.

In the worst of the bombing, Francesca went home from time to time to Somerset, and Hans sheltered from the flying bombs in the claustrophobic London Underground. When he was working for the British war effort in the north London factory, he must have heard of the bombing of Dresden on February 14th, 1945. His mother, in Dresden throughout the war, in fact survived the bombing and took refuge later in the home of a former maid, but Hans waited long for news. Correspondence with his mother restarted after the war, and she made a decision to go to South America and join her elder son. On her way she came to Paris. Hans, who had the warmest memories of his mother, must have had mixed feelings regarding a visit from her to London, where his life style was so bleak and impoverished, and he could not get to Paris to see her. In her own flight from the Russian Zone she had no passport, only a Red Cross identification card, so she could not easily come on a visit to England. And Hans had no passport at all. So his mother travelled to South America without seeing her son, and they never met again. Erna Coper died in Uruguay in 1969. Soon after the war ended, however, Hans had received from Germany a parcel of table napkins, embroidered with a Coper emblem and a single silver engraved napkin ring. These were the only tangible things to remind him of Dresden and his family.

The peace brought little change to Hans's circumstances. He carried on drawing and painting, winding armatures during the day. He worked too quickly for the peace of mind of his colleagues, and did not enjoy the control the factory had over his life. One afternoon he went to the cinema to see 'Gone With the Wind', and stayed to see the film through twice: the next day he lost his job. There were many self-help organisations in London after the war, run by refugees and emigrés, and they provided a network of contacts which helped the bewildered and rootless. One man, William Ohly, ran an art gallery near Berkeley Square, and later made an art centre at Cockfosters Abbey in Middlesex. Someone must have put Hans in contact with William Ohly, and Hans told him of his ambitions to be a sculptor, as well as his need for a job. Mr Ohly knew of a small workshop in Paddington which was in need of labour to make ceramic buttons. It was run by a refugee potter from Vienna whose name was Lucie Rie. Hans went to see her.

3 Albion Mews

Since 1939, for more than half her life, Lucie Rie has lived and worked in a small house in Albion Mews, Paddington. In the 1970s and 1980s it has become famous as the source of her celebrated and distinctive pottery, as well as the early work of Hans Coper. In a changing world it has hardly changed at all, the upstairs furnished with Mrs Rie's own furniture from Vienna designed by Ernst Plischke in the 1930s. Downstairs is the pottery workshop, including electric kilns and display shelves. When Hans Coper arrived at the door he found inside several assistants and a great deal of activity. The mews house was licensed as a factory, and was making individual glazed ceramic buttons for haute couture and for clothing manufacturers. There was a slogan in England: 'Britain can make it...', and the new socialist government was bravely building up manufacturing industry with exhortations and, sometimes, a little aid. For Lucie Rie it was a matter of survival. Her pre-war pottery in Vienna had brought her medals and distinction, but European culture and art was neither understood nor welcome in England, and she was starting from scratch, making what she was told to make.

Hans had no experience of pottery – he had never even thought about it to that date – but she took him on as one of a handful of assistants and he was paid three pounds ten shillings a week. Lucie remembers his starved appearance, and his obvious poverty, but also showing in his face was a quite indestructible self-respect retained through the war years, and he was an extraordinarily good-looking young man.

Hans made buttons at first, by the press-moulded method, in which shapes were pressed out in clay from a master mould. The holes for the thread were put in with a needle and then individually smoothed, so the thread was not abraded: a labour-intensive exercise, not unlike the winding of armatures – but the atmosphere was worlds away. Many of the workers in the pottery were refugees from Germany and Austria, but not all; there was a French girl, Colette du Plessis, and a Japanese girl, as well as Kitty Rix and Ralph Meyer, both from Vienna. The personnel changed from time to time, but working with a handful of fellow assistants in an atelier with creative intentions made all the difference to Hans's state of mind. He learned quickly about clay. He wanted to use it to make pottery and sculpture. He asked Lucie to teach him to throw on the wheel, but she advised him instead to go to a local art school, Woolwich Polytechnic, where the respected potter Heber Matthews was the instructor. Hans amazed Lucie by coming back after only a few days with the technique learned. He was thus able to play a more important part in the Albion Mews pottery, making buttons in the morning, pots in the afternoon, and drawing in the evening.

Hans was a quiet, contemplative young man, and Lucie recognised in him a broad intelligence and creative potential as well as immense charm. She simply watched as his talent as a potter grew. Because she is nearly twenty years older than Hans, and was a potter of much experience when he arrived, it has often been said and written that Hans was her pupil, even protégé, and this description quite rightly irritates her. Hans was never her pupil, not even her apprentice. At an amazingly early stage she found that she was learning from him, reacting to his views of her work, and regarding him as a creative partner, not an executant of her wishes. He was only a protégé in the strictly literal sense, since Albion Mews provided him with a refuge as well as a work place, a shelter as well as a studio. Coming to Albion Mews completely changed his life: instead of aimlessly drifting, constrained to work to keep his young family together, he could now afford to contemplate the future knowing that he had work space in which to put his ideas into practice. The year was 1946.

Hans in the Albion Mews pottery.

At first Hans was not a dynamic presence in the pottery. Often deep in thought, he was a mere shadow in the background, shy and quiet as a mouse. After he had been there about a year another German refugee came to the door, sent by William Ohly. It was Jupp Dernbach. He, too, was taken on, much to Hans's delight, for the friendship which started in the Huyton internment camp was of the kind that never falters. Jupp had regarded Hans as an avant-garde intellectual in the Army days; now he found that they shared practical mechanical skills and they worked side by side, with Jupp more demonstrative and outgoing, Hans quieter but gaining confidence and showing to his immediate work-companions a special wry wit.

For the other assistants who came and went during this vibrant period, it was a memorable time. It was the springtime of Albion Mews, and full of hope and endeavour. Jupp remembers Hans coiling the head of a man in white clay. He also remembers abstract heads by Hans, and after the working day there were drawing sessions with the assistants taking turns as models. It is lucky that Hans's sketch books have survived, and it is a pleasure to be able to include drawings from this time. The photograph above right, taken outside the house in Albion Mews, shows a confident Hans, dressed like an English undergraduate, on the left, next to Lucie, with three other helpers on the right. It was probably taken about 1948.

Apart from the button makers and the button buyers, there were many visitors to Albion Mews. Lucie Rie's contacts were widespread, and since her arrival in Britain in 1938 she had made a circle of friends including people who were to play an important part in Hans's career: Ernst Freud from Vienna; Henry Rothschild avidly buying work for his new craft shop; Muriel Rose, owner of The Little Gallery, off Sloane Street, and by this time an officer of the British Council with special responsibilities for craft and design; and of course Mr William Ohly himself. It is interesting how Lucie's visitors reacted to Hans at the beginning of his career, especially Bernard Leach. Bernard Leach of St Ives had had quite a name in Vienna even in the 1930s, and Lucie Rie had made herself known to him soon after her arrival as a refugee. Although he had not understood her pottery, and was to all intents and purposes unconcerned by European developments in ceramics, Bernard Leach obviously found Lucie herself a charming and interesting woman, and often visited Albion Mews when he was in London. Though he was aware of Hans amongst

The nucleus of the work force at Albion Mews: Hans on the left next to Lucie, and on her left Kitty Rix and Jupp Dernback from Germany with Tommy Sonnensheim in the foreground.

Round and about the new kiln at Albion Mews can be seen some of the domestic ware designs which Lucie and Hans developed in the late 1940s.

the assistants in the workshop, it was a very long time before he could do more than shake his head over Hans's work, which was so remote in mood and spirit from his own.

By 1948 most of Hans's time in the workshop was taken up in making domestic stoneware, cups and saucers designed by Lucie, fired in the newly installed stoneware kiln. At first his own pots, made after working hours, were quite small, soft in outline but boldly decorated with linear designs in white and dark brown. He threw bowls as vehicles for decoration (a concept he later rejected), and experimented with a 'new' white clay called 'T' material. Jupp Dernbach remembers Hans's excitement when Francesca's second child was born – a son whom they called Laurens. Hans never had much respect for ritualised festivals, but all his life he liked to mark personal events and dates of personal significance. Thus he threw a great bowl when his son was born, and called it 'Laurens'. It was decorated inside with a powerful design in black and white. Henry Rothschild took the bowl to his Primavera Gallery and sold it.

About this time Hans and Jupp used their engineering skills to help design a new and larger kiln for Lucie, a top-loader (used to the present day) with a frighteningly heavy lid and a device for raising and lowering it without too much effort. One weekend when Lucie went on a short visit to Vienna in the late 1940s Hans and Jupp had a clandestine firing of the new kiln they had helped to instal, to see what they could produce. It was an unhappy experiment – the kiln was overfired and the glazes ran down – but they were experimenting by themselves, using their own initiative and making their own glazes.

Three of many drawings of Angela Demmer made by Hans at Albion Mews.

In 1948, a Rumanian potter called Angela Demmer came to Albion Mews, and Hans was immediately struck with her unusual beauty. Lucie more or less turned Angela away, being in need of no more help, but Hans persuaded Lucie to let Angela come and pot in the evenings and during those weekends when Lucie was not there. Angela acted as his model, and he drew her many times, later making up a portrait bust of her which survives to this day. It clearly shows the part-African, part-European elements in her unusual face, as do the drawings, some of which are shown here. Hans kept pottery and sculpture well separated in his mind and would grumble to Angela that sculpture, not repeat-throwing, was his ambition and his destiny. Apart from heads, Hans made a figure on a horse, prepared to be fired as a 'white terracotta'. This horse and rider never reached the kiln, for Hans opened a book to find a Marino Marini horse and rider staring out at him, and he destroyed his own, for fear of being thought a plagiarist. Howard Mason, Hans's old friend from the Pioneer Corps, came to see him at Albion Mews to find that he was already producing sculpture and earning a living in a related medium which he, Howard, really knew nothing about.

The most significant and influential visitors in those years, however, were Muriel Rose and Henry Rothschild. Muriel for recognising and promoting Hans's original talent and later broadcasting it in her book *Artist Potters in England*, and Henry Rothschild for buying, then displaying, then selling Hans's work in his gallery Primavera. Thus in the late 1940s Hans Coper had pots on display when many potters only two or three years into their careers could never have hoped to get a showing. It is hard to believe today that the small group of people interested in ceramics in post-war Britain were so steeped in the Orientalism of Bernard Leach and his friends from Japan that it took a fair amount of courage to risk a critical reputation by showing such a potter as Hans Coper, whose work seemed uncomfortably abrasive to the traditionalists. The initial and unwavering support from Muriel Rose and Henry Rothschild in their different ways was of great importance, and to these two, one a communicator, the other an impresario, must go the credit for having discovered Hans Coper, in the sense that they took his work on board their own vehicles of promotion.

But it was William Ohly who first gave Hans Coper a major airing to the public, in the Autumn of 1950. The Berkeley Gallery in Davies Street, off Berkeley

Square, was a small but very prestigious setting for Hans's first exhibition, shared with Lucie Rie and, amazingly enough, the figurine sculptor Audrey Blackman. Writing about the exhibition in *Art News and Review*, Carol Hogben was overwhelmed with excitement, presumably because a pottery show in a Fine Art gallery was a rarity and what he saw did not at all conform with what he was expecting from mere potters: 'Modernism . . . here and there a surprisingly small twist which leads to an actually new form, such as the round bowls with oval levelled brim' (sic). If Carol Hogben's enthusiasm comes out in muddled prose, at least the Berkeley show was not unnoticed, and it was approved of by the Establishment. Also the reviewer saw a common feature in the work of both Lucie Rie and Hans Coper – sgraffito. 'Madame Rie . . . occasionally uses delicate criss-cross sgraffiti work. Coper's sgraffiti is free, slashing, and effective, reminding one occasionally of near-Eastern prehistoric ware.'

Sgraffito still features prominently in Lucie Rie's work, but it is and always has been repetitive, geometric and intended to create a texture. For Hans the sgraffito of this period is creative, abstract draughtsmanship on the pot, a network of lay lines, emphasising the three-dimensional shape, cut across the form and darkened by rubbing in manganese dioxide. The large vases of this first exhibition do have a link with neolithic pottery form, but they also relate to the predominant style of the great creative event of the period – the Festival of Britain in 1951.

Left: a stoneware jug by Hans Coper exhibited at the homes and gardens pavilion of the Festival of Britain. Below: 'Festival' pots illustrated in Harper's Bazaar, February 1952. The distinctive character of Hans's later work is beginning to appear.

This official gathering together of industrial and architectural designs, brainchild of Herbert Morrison and great-grandchild of the much larger and greater Great Exhibition of 1851, was supposed to prove that Britain had lost nothing of its inventiveness and had gained a good deal in terms of clarity of thought since the nineteenth century. The Royal Festival Hall is its permanent monument. Indeed it was a wonderful event, but it was at the time the subject of amused comment that a great many of the participating artists in this British Festival had names like Feliks Topolski, Bronek Katz, Ernst Pollak and Misha Black. They also included Rie, Dernbach and Coper. Hans's contribution to the Festival display was domestic stoneware, not too stark for somewhat timid English tastes. Anyone born in 1920 within a short train ride of Dessau would have grown up with the styles of the Modern Movement, but Britain still had to come to terms with continental European theories of design which had been explored elsewhere twenty years

before. Hans's pots caught the spirit of the Festival perfectly, and expressed what was best in it. After only five years' experience in ceramics, he must have felt some gratification that he had got so far so quickly. In fact he also felt a degree of frustration. Pottery, after all, was not sculpture, and he advertised his services as a sculptor in the *New Statesman* magazine. He got a reply from a retired ballet dancer in North Curry in Somerset, who was investing a great deal of money in an experimental school. Hans travelled to Somerset, which was, as far as he was concerned, one of England's best-trodden counties, and he was appointed teacher of sculpture. The trouble with the Takoma School, as it was called, was that it had more members of staff than pupils. The roll call of *alumni* never, it seems, exceeded five or six, apart from the children of members of staff, and of course these included Hans and Francesca's daughter and young son.

Hans cannot have regarded the Takoma experiment as anything other than an artificial and crazy dream, but something tempted him to take on the job, and Francesca and the two children were installed there, the Stoke Newington flat was given up, and Hans even encouraged Angela Demmer to go from London with him to teach pottery.

Hans may have felt that his health would benefit from a spell in the country – an interlinked chain of illnesses had affected him and depressed him ever since the war; pneumonia, pleurisy, jaundice; then hepatitis and TB, the latter subsequently cured, so Hans believed, after an encounter with a faith healer. It is more likely, however, that he simply wanted to get away from Stoke Newington, where the flat was too small for him to work, and the train ride too long from the Paddington workshop of Lucie Rie. The train ride from Paddington to Somerset was, of course, much longer and more costly, and Hans characteristically kept his options open by continuing to work for Lucie during the week, staying at Albion Mews, and commuting to Somerset as and when required. During this short period his family and family life suffered a good deal of neglect, and the children who were supposed to be educated at the Takoma School (though Laurens was still an infant) had to learn self-reliance and to do without their father. Francesca, virtually back on home ground in the West Country, had been acting as a 'house mother' at the North Curry school, but when this educational experiment collapsed after a visit from the education officer she had to shift for herself and her children. She rented, for £3 per week,

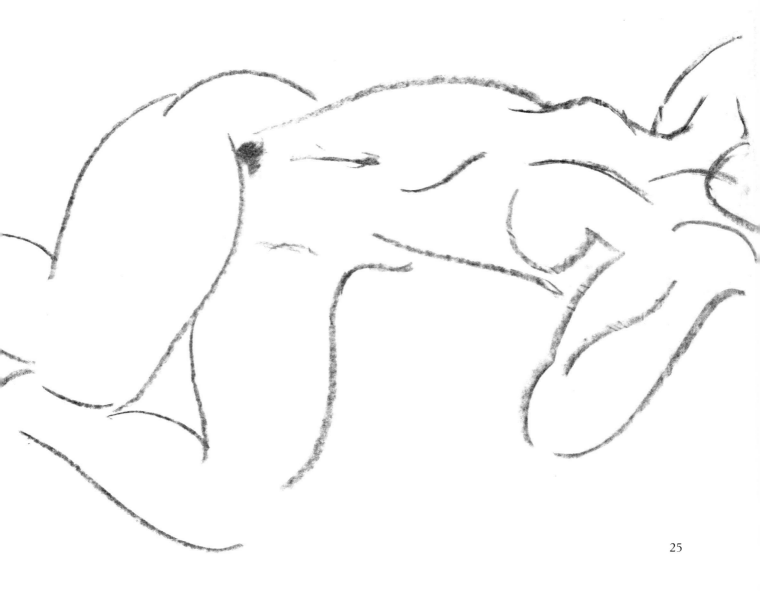

a farmhouse called Bachelor's Hall in the middle of Dartmoor. Hans came down from London for Christmas 1951 and, isolated by heavy snow from London and his work, actually spent a holiday getting to know his own children, then aged seven and three. The drawing below shows Hans's daughter, Anya, made about this time.

As the working link with Lucie Rie had never been broken, the demise of the Takoma experiment and the retreat from the West Country led naturally back to London, where Hans and Francesca moved into a Belsize Park flat found for them by the Viennese architect Ernst Freud. Friend to many and remembered

Hans the father, with his son Laurens in the garden of the Stoke Newington flat.

with great affection, Ernst Freud encouraged Hans in his work and told him to increase his prices. Hans's pattern of working increased in intensity, and he had a small windowless room at the back of the new flat which he used as a studio, and which the children were often too nervous to enter – unless they were acting themselves as models. Albion Mews, however, was still the centre of Hans's creative activity, and his friendship with Lucie had become the most important stabilising force in his life. The 1951 contribution to the Festival of Britain had been followed by an exhibit in the Milan Triennale in the same year, and articles in magazines such as *Architectural Review* drew the attention of interior designers to his work.

The narrative so far has been a chronicle of Hans's life, and shortly will return to this theme, but as the

Anya.

work which this book is designed to illustrate is now beginning to emerge, it is an appropriate point to look at what he was producing and to seek for sources. Hans had no experience of craft potteries, nor of industrial ceramics, nor even the Meissen works near to his home town of Dresden. No ceramic tradition lay round about him to affect his development. His interest at this time lay in the sculptors of the twentieth century, especially Arp and Brancusi, and in the ancient art he could find in museums. In the early post-war years he often visited the British Museum – to keep warm – where he saw collections of Egyptian, Cycladic, Etruscan and neolithic art. William Ohly's Berkeley Gallery in Davies Street introduced him to African pottery and tribal art from around the world, as well as Hellenic ceramics. Temperamentally and historically distanced from the ornate sculpture and pottery of the nineteenth and early twentieth century, with their emphasis on decoration, Hans's work at the germinal stage reflects the simplicity of primitive ceramics in which abstract decoration follows the form of the pot, as well as the work of Brancusi and the anonymous sculptors of the Cyclades. These related influences stayed with Hans throughout his creative career, and became even more strongly reflected in his own work at a later date. Pilgrim Wetton, a friend from Hans's earliest days in England, visited him at Albion Mews, and brought him an Egyptian pot from a London sale room. This ovoid pot of great simplicity became an important touchstone for Hans. He 'tuned in' to it emotionally; though separated from its humble origin by some 7000 years, he was able to relate to it and the culture from which it sprang.

In the 1950s he worked 'in reaction' to Lucie's pottery, which he admired, but he was uninfluenced and unmoved by any other modern potter's work. As he was more interested in contemporary sculptors than in pottery, he was thus strangely uncomfortable when, after the Christmas on Dartmoor, he found himself in Devon for the second time in six months, this time as a delegate with Lucie Rie at the International Conference of Craftsmen at Dartington Hall in the Summer of 1952.

In the 1950s the crafts in Britain were firmly in the grip of a small middle-class coterie, presided over by Bernard Leach. It was not until the later sixties and seventies that potters and students from a wider social spectrum were able to occupy the centre of the stage in British ceramics, without first gaining the approval of the Establishment. Bernard Leach was preaching the

Drawing for sculpture.

doctrine of excellence, at one and the same time elevating the activity of the potter to Fine Art by invoking Oriental philosophy, and glorifying the humility of the craftsman who never lifted his nose more than an inch from the clay. Taught by Howard Mason to see all art forms in a broad European context, and encouraged by the free spirit of Albion Mews, Hans found the Dartington conference an unwelcome revelation of British attitudes. The introductory speech opening the conference by Leonard Elmhirst, co-founder of Dartington Hall, set the tone for an introspective, earnest, but largely self-satisfied conclave which threatened, every time Bernard Leach got to his feet, to become an East-West dialogue, as if the entire world consisted of Japan and England, with an occasional nod of recognition in the direction of the United States, a country well represented at the conference. There were lectures with such titles as 'The Japanese Approach to the Craft' and 'The Integration of the Craftsman', interspersed with discussion groups and demonstrations. Hans found this ten-day long session amid the green lawns of Dartington tedious and depressing. Typically he made no contribution in the discussions, and kept his views and thoughts to himself. Although

Hans looks pensive in this historic picture from the Dartington Conference. On the left is Miss Muriel Rose, to the right of Hans are Kathleen Pleydell-Bouverie, Bernard Leach and Lucie Rie.

only thirty-two he must have felt more experienced and more broad-minded than many of the senior speakers, and he resolved to keep clear of associations of craftsmen in the future. One day at Dartington, however, the sun broke through when a lecture was given on 'Children' by Robin Tanner, the etcher and educationalist. In the transcript of the conference this lecture stands out for its wit and breadth of vision. Hans attended and enjoyed it, and became friends with the lecturer, another friendship which lasted until Hans's death.

He returned from Dartington in 1952 determined to plough his own furrow, and in the sanctuary of the Albion Mews pottery started to develop a range of rather jagged shapes, with coarse linear patterns in white and black or simply blackened on the outside with a heavy coating of manganese dioxide. As already mentioned, the only ceramic influence on Hans was Lucie Rie, and when he said that he made his own pottery 'in reaction' to her he was only half-serious. In fact the two collaborated closely on the domestic ware which occupied so much time in the 1940s and early '50s, with Lucie designing the shapes and executing the decoration, and Hans throwing the ware, subtly modifying the shape and adding some of the handles. Only an expert can distinguish a Hans Coper coffee cup from a Lucie Rie coffee cup, but Lucie herself recognised the contribution he was making to the aes-

thetic qualities of her work, and insisted that much of the joint domestic ware should bear a joint imprint. Thus on the underside of certain highly prized items of tableware are to be found the two seals alongside each other. The photographs opposite show some of the ware, and the pictures below them show the seals. Such was the closeness with which Hans and Lucie were now working that Hans was involved in cutting (and slightly modifying) the celebrated LR seals, as

Lucie and Hans in front of the Albion Mews pottery in the early 1950s.

Above and right : tableware made jointly by Lucie Rie and Hans Coper.

well as his own, and many seals in plaster and biscuit-fired clay were produced in different sizes by Hans.

Potters' seals do not always give much indication of the pottery or the potter, but these two, LR and HC, are so beautiful in themselves and so well matched to the work as to give a frisson of pleasure to most collectors and admirers when a pot is turned up and the seal revealed. This is not merely the pleasure of recognition and identification, for pots by Hans were readily recognisable as unique and original by the beginning of the 1950s. He was beginning to create a completely new visual vocabulary in ceramics.

If one has to seek for sources of inspiration in Hans's early work one must look to sculptors, even painters, rather than potters, and in particular the work of Constantin Brancusi and Marino Marini. Picasso, Gabo and Matisse seemed to him like giants, each with a coiled spring of energy; but Hans found inspiration too in the folk art sculpture of Africa and the Americas, that unegotistical art which inches its way towards the ultimate development of a simple theme, and at the same time captures and retains in each piece an element of the 'essence'. In the early 1950s Picasso, Braque and Ben Nicholson were a strong influence on Hans in the decoration of pots with semi-figurative or abstract designs, as the pictures on pages 91 and 97 show. A straightforward figurative design such as that on the small bowl on the next page is very rare, if not unique,

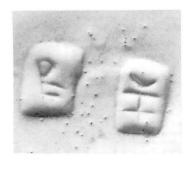

Left : an early Coper seal. Right : the base of a pot bearing both Hans's and Lucie's seals.

Small bowl, 12 cm diameter, owned by Angela Demmer.

and it dates from the period of the ill-fated Marino Marini horse.

Abstracted heads in fired clay from the mid 1950s survive, as shown on page 33, but Hans was inclined to abandon solid clay sculpture before he had finished it, and much was consigned to Lucie Rie's attic, including unfinished heads of herself. By great good fortune, the most complete head of Lucie, dating from the mid 1950s, was found undamaged and uncracked in 1981. It has now been cast and is illustrated on page 32: a sensitive and moving tribute to this fertile period of both their careers.

Hans was later to say that clay was the most intractable and unresponsive of all the media, and that he never enjoyed working with it, as some potters and sculptors do. Nevertheless, in a period of less than ten years he had gained a complete control over it, and was using clay and nothing else. It was for him very much a naked confrontation with a single material which would show one's every mistake and mark. In order to gain a satisfactory end product, most potters are manipulating several facets of their craft at once, usually to their advantage by allowing one to take over from the other in times of difficulty: clay, glass or glaze and the kiln itself make a composite whole. Hans knew what he wanted to achieve, and went to it without help from glaze or kiln. It should be said, especially for those unfamiliar with pottery techniques, that while most pottery is twice fired, once for the body

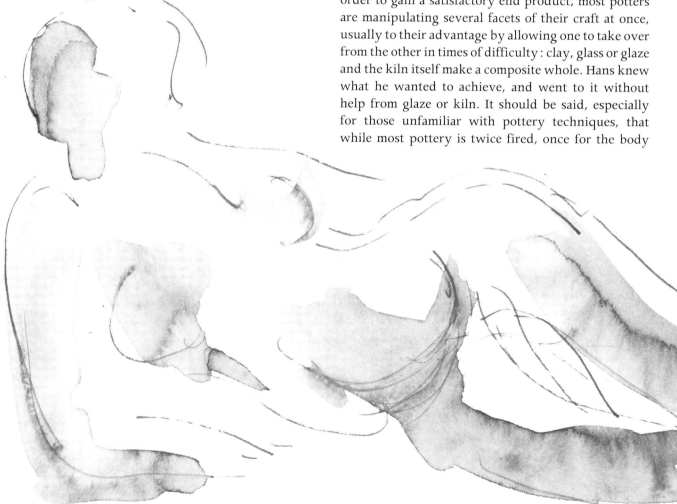

material and once for the glaze decoration coat, the Lucie Rie pottery adopted the unusual technique of putting work only once through the kiln. Hans followed suit – indeed at Albion Mews he had little choice, for the system was economical of fuel, and the one prescribed for all tableware. The implications as far as his work is concerned are considerable. The application of the surface glaze, or slip, coat to an unfired pot requires dexterity and some courage. It is also much more easily achieved with a brush than by spraying or by dipping the pot in the glaze. The application of several coats of slip or colouring oxide to an unfired pot can be carried out rather after the manner of a French polisher, where by laborious means you can achieve a cherished result. These methods cannot be used to the same effect on conventional biscuit-fired pottery.

The surface of Hans's pots, developed in the 1950s and refined throughout his career, is the result of sanding, scratching, painting and staining, then starting the process all over again, and the final form and the surface have a harmony which differs from that of other potters' work. In Hans's case the surface is more like the patina given by time, as on the handle of a well-used garden spade, but controlled so that there is nothing accidental about the surfaces and shadows. Manganese is the key constituent, mixed in oxide form with gum arabic and a little iron oxide to make the black surface which vitrifies in the kiln if it is thickly applied to the pot, and the clay used was always based on white 'T' material, with its grainy 'tooth' like a canvas. Very early beaker-like shapes were glazed experimentally with a honey-coloured glaze, and some had impressed and incised patterns,

Self-portrait.

Portrait head of Lucie Rie, c. 1953.

emphasised by manganese oxide. These pots, called 'treacle pots' by Lucie, are illustrated on page 84, and are extremely rare. The reason why they are rare is that they were only tests, and it is hard to decide if they have a place in the survey of Hans Coper's work, since inclusion is bound to squeeze out something else. They are included because they are so beautiful.

By about 1953 the finely incised lines of the Festival of Britain ware, which had appealed to Muriel Rose, had begun to be replaced by stronger semi-figurative designs in white against a black ground, achieved by painting manganese on the surface, scraping through to the white clay, then glazing in white with a Lucie Rie glaze of orange-peel surface, through which the dense manganese burnt a dark, metallic, Vandyke brown. A good example of this is the well known jug shown opposite, and also the bowls on pages 92–3.

In 1953 Hans contributed to an exhibition of British potters in the Stedelijk Museum in Amsterdam, and in the same year there was another exhibition shared with Lucie Rie at the Berkeley Gallery, opened by George Wingfield-Digby of the Victoria and Albert Museum, followed by a prize-winning exhibit in the Milan Triennale (see page 86), and though Hans was earning his living by making domestic ware for Lucie Rie, working for exhibitions was also beginning to be an important and motivating feature of his life. Regular sales, especially to Henry Rothschild's Primavera Gallery and occasional private buyers, plus publicity in magazines such as *Harper's Bazaar* and *Architectural Review*, meant that by 1955 his work was being seen as far afield as Gothenburg in Sweden and Bonniers on Madison Avenue in New York. Mr Holmquist of this store was already acting as an agent for Lucie Rie, and he mounted a one-man show of Hans's work in the Spring of 1956.

Hans did not travel to America for the event, for he had no passport and could not afford the luxury of travel. Instead he moved house. The home environment in the Belsize Park flat with Francesca and the two children had been under strain for some time. The children, by now ten years and six years old respectively, were attractive, happy looking children, but taking care of them was quite enough for Francesca, and quite beyond Hans. After more than ten years with Francesca, Hans moved away to a small flat in Bloomsbury.

The list of exhibitions which featured Hans's work at this time might give the impression that he was moving steadily towards a fulfilling career. But in fact

Semi-abstract heads in high-fired white clay, early 1950s.

Stoneware jug with sgraffito design through manganese dioxide, 29 cm high, c. 1952. Collection of Henry Rothschild.

the mid '50s were a time of great struggle, with the added financial pressures of three children to support : his marriage to Penelope had been dissolved in 1952, but the child's maintenance continued. The small flat in which he lived alone in Rugby Chambers, Bloomsbury, was very austere. On a piece of plywood which blocked up the fireplace Hans carefully wrote in Roman capitals, 'AT TU CATULLE DESTINATUS OBDURA' – *Endure your own destiny*. I cannot help wondering if Hans was referring to his destiny in general, or if the quotation should be taken in the context of Catullus's own unrequited love – or indeed if the quotation had any relevance at all, for it might have been merely a typographical exercise. One of the things that Hans was enduring, however, at this time was the stiffening of his upper spine, now diagnosed

as *spondylitis ankylosa* which gave him a characteristically stiff-necked, hunched posture discernible in the
early photograph shown right, taken by Jane Gate, a
young photographer who later became his wife. Jane
had met Hans and visited the Albion Mews pottery
when she was just beginning a course in photography
at the London School of Printing, and she found in
Hans an excellent and surprisingly willing model for
portrait photographs. It is thus that there exist very
numerous photographs of the handsome thirty-five-
year-old, and almost continuous records of his pottery
from 1955 onwards. It is interesting to compare some
of the photographs of this time and later with the
monochrome self-portrait on canvas which Hans drew
and gave to Lucie, as illustrated on page 90, and also
with his drawing on page 31.

Hans had by 1955 almost abandoned sculptural
work and was concentrating on pots. Even the open
decorated bowls were beginning to be phased out by
a concentration on bulbous forms and curving, waisted
vases. Critics would use words like 'masculine' or even
'male' to describe his work. Actually they were at a
loss for words, or at least those brought up on Bernard
Leach were, for Hans Coper's pots did not fit into any
ready-made categories. They were not complicated
shapes, and to call them 'new' would be to imply a
naivety which any critic fears. So they were called
'rugged' or 'male'. The pots of this time were certainly
sensual. Unlike the organic asymmetrical shapes of
pots by Ruth Duckworth, another German refugee and
Hans's exact contemporary, who was working independently in London, Hans's pots were bulbous and
yet trim: enough to make a maiden blush without
knowing quite why. The illustrations on pages 122 and
123 show how these shapes relate to one another, and
most were made from a single unaltered thrown shape,
sanded, scrubbed, slipped and scrubbed again to a fine

finish with no superfluous decoration. Size and weight were carefully related; many of the pots of this time are very large and heavy, and have the air of being ritual objects. Jugs are anthropomorphic, vases tall and waisted. Just a few of the larger pots of this time were beginning to show the bi-symmetry of the later work which comes from a combination of two shapes, and the characteristic combining of flat disc shapes set on edge within a standing form (see page 81).

Two important private collectors appeared in Hans's life about this time. Mr William Ismay from Wakefield, who came direct to Albion Mews, and Mr J.M.W. Crowther of Wimbledon, a painter who always attended any exhibition of Hans's work and with a receptive and intelligent eye bought a great many of the pots. Hans's pleasure at seeing how well his pots were selling from galleries turned to wry disappointment when he found that they were mainly being sold to one man.

At Albion Mews, the button factory of the 1940s had given way to an efficient pottery, and most of the assistants of the early days had disappeared. Jupp Dernbach left the pottery to concentrate on mosaics after the Festival of Britain, and all the refugees had gone. Hans's friend Angela Demmer had left to live in Paris, and at her invitation Hans made his first post-war trip abroad, at the end of 1956. He and Jane Gate travelled to Paris to stay with Angela, and to meet Hans's idol, Constantin Brancusi. Angela was friendly with the experimental sculptor Tinguely, who used a studio next door, and she was an occasional visitor to Brancusi, but unfortunately for Hans the hoped-for meeting never quite took place. Brancusi was ill and in bed in his studio, and Hans did not get beyond the doorway. It was New Year's Day 1957, and by March Brancusi was dead. To get as close as he did, however, was a moving experience for Hans, who saw the legendary Brancusi works in situ, including the various versions of the Endless Column which stood like totems in the high studio. While in Paris Hans and Jane also visited the French potter Francine Del Pierre, who remained a friend until her death in 1968.

The visit to Paris may have stimulated Hans to paint and draw again, and after his return he experimented for a short time with a graphic process based on leather-hard clay. As far as I know, it is quite unique. He carved designs into flattened slabs of clay, much as a lino cutter cuts lino, though of course the clay is softer and the drawing more supple. By rolling waterbound ink gently on to the clay and pressing the

With Francine Del Pierre in her Paris studio, 1956.

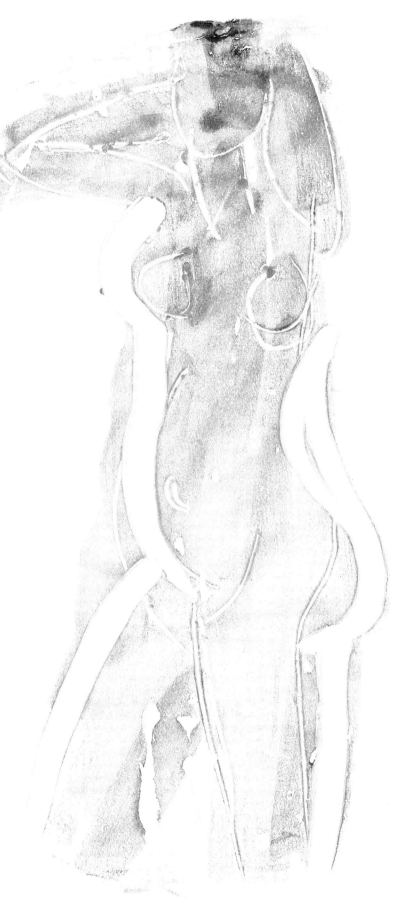

result against a sheet of glass he was able to take prints from the glass in the manner of monotypes. Four or five prints could come from each subject before re-inking, and Hans made occasional changes to the 'master cuts' as an etcher does to his plate.

Jane remembers him working on the clay graphics, but the whole episode only occupied about a month, and Hans put the prints away in a drawer, apart from one which was mounted on the wall. The drawings are influenced by Picasso and Matisse, but the prints have an expressive and haunting quality like the woodcuts of Emil Nolde, and some are reproduced on these pages.

In 1957, Hans worked with Lucie on a joint exhibition in America at the University of Minnesota, and was then offered his first one-man show at Primavera, Sloane Street, by Henry Rothschild. The exhibition in early 1958, with over a hundred pieces, was a remarkable success and is well documented. Some of the pots are illustrated on pages 98 and 99. All this work had to be made in the Albion Mews studio, and although Lucie had at no time felt Hans was occupying too much of her pottery, the studio was beginning to be too small for both of them. It was then that Hans Coper received a communication from a certain Henry Morris, who

had had the dream of creating an art centre on the edge
of the Hertfordshire town of Welwyn Garden City. He
had found a building, a large Georgian house called
Digswell House, and as secretary of the Digswell Arts
Trust Henry Morris wrote to Hans to offer him a studio
and living accommodation at Digswell. Thus again he
was to be a pioneer, and a somewhat reluctant one,
but for Hans it was the opportunity of a large studio
of his own, and freedom to experiment. He gave up
the London flat in Bloomsbury, gently withdrew his
roots from the Albion Mews workshop that had suc-
coured him for so long, and moved out of town on
January 1st, 1959.

Pots in the Digswell studio, a photograph taken in 1960.

4 The Digswell Years

By the time of the inauguration of the Digswell Arts Trust in May 1959, Hans had been in residence for five months, and he hid behind the Sadia water heater in his flat when Lady Mountbatten came round the studios to view the artists on the opening day. There were at the time some thirteen artists and their families in residence, and Hans's evasive action is remembered with great glee by his contemporaries, because this seemed somehow so characteristic. He was not being impolite – constant politeness is one of the things about Hans which casual friends remember best – he simply wanted to avoid awkward or pointless conversation. He disliked formal occasions, pomp and ceremony, and above all he disliked being on show.

The Digswell Arts Trust had been set up as the brainchild and dream of Henry Morris, who had been Director of Education for Cambridgeshire until 1954, an educationalist of vision by then retired and living in Hertfordshire. Henry Morris had strong views about the effect of mechanisation and the machine on standards, and particularly on standards of design, and he spent the last years of his life trying to ensure that artists made a contribution which was taken up and used by society at large, rather than neglected.

In the introduction to the Digswell prospectus he wrote:

> The prototypes of the articles that are manufactured by the thousand *must* be designed by artists . . . the practice ought to be one of the unquestioned assumptions of our industry and culture. . . . What is taking place creatively at the hands of living artists in contemporary life is the flowering point of art. . . . What we have to do is to relate the artist and the craftsman in a realistic way to the community.

Henry Morris had a wide range of contacts, especially in the field of architecture; he had persuaded Walter Gropius to design Impington Village College in Cambridgeshire in the 1930s, before Gropius went to America. Now the opportunity to turn the empty and redundant Digswell House into a work centre for artists seemed a heaven-sent chance to put his ideas into practice. The accommodation for the artists was to be cheap and basic, with the emphasis on working space. Prospective artists and craftsmen would go before a selection panel, but the first three artists engaged were 'hors concours', and they were Ralph Brown, sculptor, Peter Collingwood, weaver, and Hans Coper. Henry Morris offered Hans a flat and a studio for £3 per week, and Hans and Lucie went to see the bare buildings in 1958. The photograph below shows Hans with Morris in the glazed porch of his future house.

Most of the inmates lived in flats in the Georgian mansion, with studios on the periphery, but Hans had his studio attached to a separate small house of which he occupied the ground floor. He was therefore insulated somewhat from the main community, and worked and lived quite alone until an upstairs flat was prepared for Donald Brook, an experimental sculptor who came to live there with his wife, Phyllis. At thirty-nine Hans was one of the oldest artists in residence. Some of the others still had their reputations to make, and had only recently left art school. Hans was regarded with some awe and a great deal of respect, based both on his work and his personality. He lived and worked at Digswell for the best part of five years, and the work he did there was some of the most forceful and striking of his whole career. Digswell represents his maturity as an artist, as well as a significant stage in his personal development. Up to this time his friends and colleagues, especially Lucie Rie, had seen him growing in stature, and still developing. The people he met at Digswell had a different view of him. To them he was already grown – a fully formed artist and mature man.

For some artists conventional family life is not just draining and inhibiting: it is intolerable; and such it was for Hans. Although he had moved about from home to home since he came to live in England, Digswell was the first time he had really had a home of his own, where his life was shared simply with his work. In consequence his commitment to ceramics deepened, and in what appeared to observers as loneliness and isolation he was able to come to terms with himself. He was visited by depression, and frequently for months at a time, yet he was intensely productive and creative. He had by now developed confidence in his work, and had the essential facility for self-criticism. He allowed pottery, or more particularly the potter's wheel, to circumscribe his efforts and he worked according to certain strict criteria, felt both intuitively and intellectually. He knew that only the artist could decide for himself or herself what needs to be done, that outside influences were irrelevant. Ultimately he had to be able to face the criticism offered back to him by his own work, and he knew that his work had only one critic – himself. He had gained what David Queensberry later described, quoting from Hermann Hesse's *Steppenwolf*, as 'that calm objectivity, that cer-

Hans with Henry Morris in the glazed porch of his future home at Digswell.

Hans's Digswell workshop is full of pots, with drawings of pots and tiles pinned to the walls. The open door leads to his living quarters: plain and bare.

tainty of thought and knowledge, as only really intellectual men have.'

Hans himself at the time would hardly have seen it that way. For him his position seemed to be an accumulation of contradictions, an ironic juxtaposition of the opportunity to work and not to work, as expressed by Goethe's dictum that 'reflection, if persisted in, results in so many opportunities for alternative action that it results in inertia' – the counterpoint of longed-for freedom with the creative paralysis that freedom brings. Yet from his arrival at Digswell work poured out from him and he set new standards both for himself and for others. Within the Digswell community he was seen as a somewhat enigmatic figure, remembered by colleagues universally with warmth and affection which has grown, not withered, in the intervening years. His environment, as at Rugby Chambers in London, was austere, but this time he created it entirely for himself. He bought and installed two electric kilns in the studio, but brought almost nothing else for home comfort. Throughout his stay the walls in the house remained their original plastered pink, his furniture was a low bed, a desk and a chair. There was his own coffee pot (possibly the only one he ever made) and a set of beautiful Lucie Rie bowls, deep and white, for coffee. This austerity was not just because of lack of resources – though he had alimony to pay and children to maintain – it was because it suited his chosen way of life. Donald Brook, who had

come to live in the flat above, commented that there would have been little difference in his way of life if he had been a wealthy man, and Donald and other Digswell residents remembered his flat as a place of barren beauty, somewhat Japanese, not of barren poverty.

Over the period of five years friendships grew with many of the artists, in particular Michael Andrews, Ralph and Caroline Brown, John Wragg, Peter Collingwood, Mary and David Noble, but it was with Donald Brook and his wife Phyllis, partly because of proximity and partly because of temperament, that the warmest friendship developed. Games of chess brought the two men together, and long evening sessions waiting for the kiln to reach temperature would be spent playing chess and, when they could afford it, drinking whisky. A mutual interest in philosophy in relation to art absorbed, in Donald's recollection, hundreds of hours of conversation, with Hans's position reflecting his interest in the writings of Kandinsky and the teaching of the Bauhaus. Hans revealed to Donald Brook his distaste for the Oriental School of English pottery which had grown up around Bernard Leach and Michael Cardew, and his dislike of heavy handmade pottery in general. He extolled the virtues of his Woolworth's crockery in terms of basic design, decoration, weight, fit of glaze and professionalism. He expressed his uncertainty regarding the 'truth to materials' doctrine of Henry Moore, and

A bronze 'pot' from 1960.

Donald Brook and Hans making a plaster mould from a huge thrown bowl.

proved this by enlisting Donald's help to make moulds for thrown pots to be cast in a cement and fibre-glass mixture and in bronze. Donald spoke of these experiments:

The bronzes he played with for some time. I don't think he was entirely satisfied with them. He considered there was something artificial about the procedure. He tried to reconcile himself to this by arguments against the truth to materials aesthetic with which he never did agree. It was his case that art was essentially artificial. He much admired Mondrian, and Mondrian's attitudes. He held that nature and art were entirely separate, so that it didn't seem to him that there was any theoretical objection to making a thing by throwing it and then perpetuating it by casting. The unnaturalness was attractive. I think he just didn't like the result. It didn't have the surface texture and finish – the delicacy that he wanted. . . . It was a strong point about his pots that they had this immense subtlety of surface. This glaze that was not a glaze, and colour that was not a colour: something that certainly couldn't be duplicated at all in bronze.

The photograph shows moulds being made for one of the large bowls he was developing as plant containers for municipal use in New Towns, and a bronze 'pot' is shown above left.

One of the first things that Hans had needed on arrival at Digswell was transport to get him back to London, to visit Lucie Rie in Albion Mews and Jane Gate, who had taken over the Bloomsbury flat. He bought a retired London taxi, an Austin heavy 12/4 of 1937 or 1938, which was uneconomical and ponderous, but had the special advantage of an upright driving position which Hans liked because of his back troubles. He took great pleasure in driving the taxi as fast as it would go. His slightly hunched, stiff-necked figure at the wheel became in 1959 and 1960 one of the familiar sights of Digswell, and in the photograph right he is seen with Lucie Rie on the way to his studio.

The taxi was sometimes parked in Albion Mews when Hans was visiting London, and on at least one occasion Hans returned to the wheel to find a fare-proffering passenger in the back, waiting to be driven home. The taxi had a special significance one day when Hans drove it to Victoria Station in 1960. He was there to meet his brother Walter, on a short business visit to London from Argentina. It was their first meeting after twenty-three years, and Walter reports with pleasure how 'he was just so as I had him in my memory . . . since the day he came with me to Hamburg [in 1937] and waved me goodbye at the pier,' but Hans thought, 'I bet he thinks I am a taximan.' Walter was driven quickly, or as quickly as was possible, to the sanctuary of Albion Mews, where the photograph below was taken, and gently introduced to the concept of his brother's being a potter. Walter Coper also visited Digswell, and although the visit to England was brief, a rapport was re-established and maintained for the next twenty years.

The taxi had a makeshift passenger seat in the front, leaving the back free for pots. In the same year of 1960 it conveyed Hans and Lucie to Yorkshire with a great many ceramic discs, designed by Hans as a mural to be installed in Swinton Secondary (now Comprehensive) School near Rotherham. This was a worthwhile commission organised through the good offices of Henry Morris; it was worth £600, but Hans had to justify himself and work hard for it. He had been called before the education committee of Yorkshire councillors, 'We are spending public money on modern art. Tell me, Mr Coper, what does it mean?' The mural consists of double discs on each side of a dividing wall between an assembly room and a hallway. Hans and Lucie Rie supervised the installation and the mural is shown on page 115, photographed in 1982.

A similar, slightly smaller, wall was commissioned by the Powell Duffryn Group and installed in the

Lucie, Hans and the taxi.

Hans's brother Walter stands between Lucie and Hans in the Albion Mews pottery in 1960. On the right is Jupp Dernbach.

entrance to their premises in Berkeley Street in 1961. Unfortunately the company moved to Berkeley Square in 1964 and the ceramic discs were rearranged to fit a new and larger wall, much to Hans's dissatisfaction. With the relative positions of the discs altered, the wall had no meaning.

The frustrations caused by conflicting interests and needs are familiar to all those who have anything to do with architecture, and the experience with the Powell Duffryn wall is, in a way, symbolic of Hans's experiences with architecture in general, which coincided with his period at Digswell House. True to the tenets of Henry Morris's introductory speech, Hans was to cooperate with an architectural group in the designing of ceramic products, and in fact Hans's livelihood at Digswell, replacing his income from working with Lucie Rie in Albion Mews, came from grants of £500 and £1000 from the Elmgrant Trust and the Maidenhead Brick and Tile Company for the production of ceramic wall cladding and acoustic bricks. Hans jokingly called Digswell his 'architectural period', and divided his time between individual wheel-made pots and designs for architects. Every six weeks the gathering of architects and representatives of building trades, calling itself the Digswell Group, assembled at Hans's studio. The sessions were to discuss the designs prepared by Hans, and how they could be manufactured and marketed. Hans genuinely welcomed the opportunity to work with industry, and was able to test out the Bauhaus principles he warmly espoused. 'Back to square one' was like being given his freedom once again, and the designs flowed out.

The drawing board, however, was turned into a chess board, in which he was constantly in check, and finally checkmated. His commercial work fell into three parts. Firstly he was to design clay-based cladding materials on the principles of eighteenth-century mathematical tiling, which would allow the infilling of prefabricated structures with overlapping tiles, to give varied surface texture and pattern from a very limited number of units. Some six or seven different tile patterns were produced, some glazed, and some biscuit clay, all extruded and in materials of different earth colours. They were launched on the market in 1961, with advertising in the trade journals, and a stand at Olympia which Hans himself designed. Hans took the whole project extremely seriously, as indeed did all the architect members of the group. He made miniature models of the tiles, and a carpentry panel outside his workshop on which to test samples as they

Phyllis and Donald Brook, and Hans.

The Powell Duffryn wall in its original location in Berkeley Street.

Hans designed an enormous range of glazed facing tiles for the SGB company in Dudley. They had low relief, as shown left, and some, far right, top and centre, were designed to provide a variety of patterns from a single tile unit.

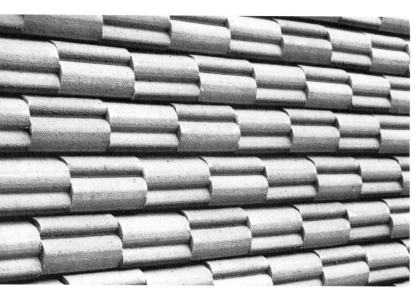

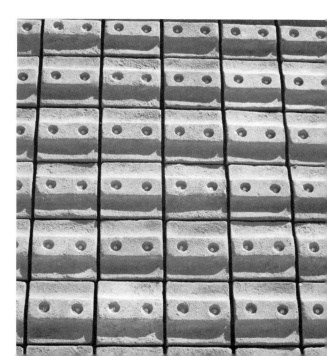

So-called mathematical tiles have been hung to imitate brickwork since Georgian times. Hans was employed to create a more varied surface by designing pairs of tiles for cladding walls, in particular for the CLASP schools of the 1960s. Two of his special designs are shown above, a variation of mathematical tiles above right. They were all made by the Keymer Tile Company of Burgess Hill, Sussex, and six sets of designs were in production in the 1960s. On the right: Hans's design for panel tiles fixed with screws.

arrived from the factory. An enormous number of photographs were taken by Jane Gate to assist in the publicity, and several of the designs are illustrated here. In the 1960s concrete and other products gave a cheaper form of cladding than ceramic materials, and the designs laboured under a cost disadvantage. The tiles were patented in the company's name, not Hans's,

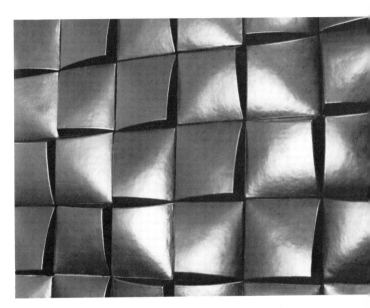

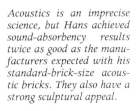

Children play outside a primary school near Mansfield, where Hans's tiles have been in use for twenty years.

Acoustics is an imprecise science, but Hans achieved sound-absorbency results twice as good as the manufacturers expected with his standard-brick-size acoustic bricks. They also have a strong sculptural appeal.

47

The Curlew washbasin.

Acoustic bricks built into the wall of a sports hall.

and after some years they were abandoned. Where they were installed they proved successful and popular (see page 47). It now seems likely that with the elevation of concrete prices in the 1980s Hans's fine designs will be reissued. The patents are held by the Keymer Tile Company, but outside Hans's Digswell home all that remained in 1983 of the sample tiles were being used as the borders for the kitchen garden.

The second project for industry over which Hans laboured for years at Digswell were designs for wash-basins and lavatory basins for the S.G.B. Company of Dudley. Donald Brook remembers clearly the rather monumental sight of white plaster prototype lavatories and basins in Hans's sparse accommodation, and both he and John Wragg remember how Hans spent months, if not years, perfecting the designs, which were finally marketed with his name attached to the publicity material and his initials H and C neatly on the taps. The design of so-called sanitary ware in Britain was not very lively in the early 1960s, and Hans's clean designs were so beautiful that they are worthy of illustration here. Examples of the little bowl christened 'The Curlew' may still be found lurking in some builders' merchant's yard, and would prove today a valuable collector's item. For Hans, however, all the pleasure and the pain was in the sculpting stage, and after giving the first sample bowls to Lucie and other friends, he forgot about them.

The third architectural project was concerned with internal cladding bricks and tiles designed for acoustic purposes. The need for permanent untarnishable sound-trapping cladding is known to anyone who visits a gymnasium or swimming pool, and Hans designed a series of sculptural units which could be installed like conventional masonry, but could accommodate sound-soaking pads of rubber or other material in their 'jaws'. They so appealed to architects that they were specified without pads as decorative walling and were also used, perhaps rather idiotically, on outside walls at London Airport in the hope that they would Hoover-up the revving roar of jet planes. Although their acoustic qualities were remarkably good, the high cost of the units finally exhausted the demand, and now the patents lie unused, with Blockley's Brick Company.

Hans's consultancy for the architectural group continued beyond his time at Digswell, though it brought him no profit. It could be said to have been born bravely in 1960, after his arrival at Digswell, and to have become moribund three years later. Commercial considerations which confronted Hans with the architectural group were such as he had never encountered before. He found the experience disillusioning. His contact with individual architects was, on the contrary, stimulating. It did not only come from Digswell, for his wartime friend Howard Mason had qualified as an architect, and an architect visitor to Lucie's pottery in Albion Mews, fired by enthusiasm for Hans's pots, introduced his work to Basil Spence, who offered to Hans his most prestigious commission to date – the design of candlesticks for Coventry Cathedral. It amused Hans that a half-Jew with no attachments to the Anglican religion should be asked to do this work, but with his usual professionalism he set about designing baluster-like shapes which were to be seven feet high when complete. He made small models, and finally executed the units in pieces, fitting them together on steel dowels. They were installed in early 1962, and the picture below shows Hans fixing the units and showing with his own body their massive scale. Some people regard them as most important works, and Jane Gate remembers well the impressive effect of this line of columns on the day they were installed, before the building became cluttered with too many other artefacts. The Coventry candlesticks led to other interesting developments. Dr Fischer of the Fischer Fine Art Gallery learned that Henry Moore admired Hans Coper's work, and commissioned a large pot by Hans in the Coventry candlesticks idiom, which was given to Henry Moore as a Christmas present. It is ironic that after Hans's pilgrimage to see Brancusi in Paris, a trip to Much Hadham to see Henry Moore

Above: two of the six candlesticks at Coventry Cathedral, and, left, Hans helping to instal them in 1962.

was similarly futile. He went unannounced, with the hope of meeting and talking to the sculptor: unlike Brancusi, Henry Moore was not ill, but was out for the day and the two men never met.

Basil Spence commissioned from Hans more candlesticks for a religious building when he designed the Meeting House at Sussex University. This time Hans conceived the shapes in bowl form, and two massive black modern pots are the result: they are superb. The Meeting House pots for Sussex University came after the end of the Digswell period (the date was about 1965), and could be said to represent the signing off of the architectural work. In this instance they were pots *for* a building, rather than as part of a building.

49

One of a pair of twin candle holders designed for the Meeting House at Sussex University, 40 cm diameter.

Right: some pots from the Crowther collection, photographed by William Ismay before they were destroyed.

Architectural activities had reduced the amount of attention Hans could give to exhibitions of his pottery during the Digswell years. He was working out ideas with great intensity, but exhibiting little, and in the chronology of his career on page 206 there is a conspicuous lack of exhibitions between 1960 and 1964. In 1959, his first year at Digswell, he had sent work to a major international exhibition at Syracuse, New York, and later in the same year to the Smithsonian Institution Travelling Exhibition. In 1960 he exhibited for the first time at Nottingham with the Midland Group, the first of several Nottingham shows to which he contributed. He made a major contribution of twelve pots, including some massive ones, to the exhibition of English potters at the Boymans Museum in Rotterdam, and private and public buyers in Holland were beginning to make collections of his work. But then it was not until 1964 when he had left Digswell that Hans contributed to another exhibition – this time in Tokyo. The work he produced and let out of his Digswell studio was mainly sold through small shops and galleries, with Henry Rothschild a frequent buyer for Primavera.

The discerning collector who had so assiduously bought pots at the Berkeley Gallery exhibitions, Mr J.M.W.Crowther, now had a collection of over fifty Coper pots, certainly the largest collection out of the artist's own hands. He made himself known to Hans, but the relationship was not a close one and Mr Crowther, when he visited Digswell, would see Hans at work in his studio and go away again without disturbing him. He could not bring himself to interrupt. He admired Hans immensely and almost worshipped his collection of pots. This is perhaps why in 1961 Mr Crowther destroyed all but one of the Copers he owned, as he felt that they were becoming too much of an obsession, and disrupting his family life. Luckily Bill Ismay had visited him and photographed the pots before this event, and some of the destroyed Copers are pictured below. This is the only instance I know of Hans's work exerting an influence best described as 'not to the good'. The soon legendary smashing up of the pots upset Lucie more than Hans himself, and in Mr Crowther's defence it should be said that what he did was supposed to be private: it was not a spectacular and symbolic act like slashing the Mona Lisa, and the thought of hurting Hans was never in his mind. The public inference, however, of some personal vendetta was inevitably drawn, and this must have been distressing for them both.

To understand better Hans's reaction, an ambivalent mixture of humour, humility and hurt, it is worth noting Donald Brook's recollection that when Hans learnt that all his pots were being bought by one man he said, 'Anyone who collects Copers must be mad'. Ralph and Carrie Brown, who worked in the adjacent studio at Digswell, appreciated Crowther's reluctance to disturb Hans at work, for when potting Hans worked with

great intensity, and a magical concentration, and having completed his pots, in families and groups, he was very reluctant to part with them. In fact, when a buyer came to take pots away at Digswell Hans would appear to grieve quietly over the empty shelves for days. This was not sentimentality. The pots were part of himself; their removal was an erosion of the artist, even a violation. Certain pots were so special to Hans that under no circumstance would he part with them, and it is fortunate for the preparation of this book that so much of his finest work is available for photography.

While at one end he would hold on to certain pots which were touchstones or marker buoys in his route, at the other he was entirely ruthless in destroying pots which did not match up to his own standards. For this reason the quality of pots from the Digswell time onwards is without exception extremely high. Certain early Albion Mews work made its way through the kiln and out of the pottery which Hans would certainly have killed off in later years. Ralph Brown remembers that at Digswell 'the discards were colossal'. It became an important principle to Hans about this time that if you were working on a series of related pots you worked to the limit of your ability, each pot nudging the next into a higher state of grace, and when the series was complete all but the best would have to be destroyed.

By this time most of Hans's pots were made by joining two or more thrown shapes, and the techniques he employed are described in the next chapter. The composite nature of the pottery broke up and lengthened the creative process. First the pieces, or parts, had to be thrown, and throwing was something Hans enjoyed. It was a pleasurable, sensual experience which contrasted with the agony of assembling the pot, as though every decision he took slotted a form permanently into recorded three-dimensional space. In conceiving his pots he was very much concerned with the space between them and around them. He often drew the outlines of pots temporarily on wet clay slabs, and it was no accident that the shapes overlapped on these low reliefs. It is clear from the photographs of his work that one shape leads to another, and echoes of early forms are seen reappearing in later pots. But Hans was also interested in the negative spatial shapes created when pots interacted, so that each individual pot has its place in a very complex pattern, like a sound or phrase in a musical composition. This tuning-up of his pots means they are never cabbagey, nor are they luscious or relaxed.

Sometimes Hans himself could relax, and the artistic community of Digswell benefited from his quiet self-deprecating wit, his love of coffee, beer, whisky, poker, and especially his love of parties. All the residents at Digswell, especially the women, remember how he loved to dance, and he clearly got great benefit and warmth from the close company of friends. It was a reciprocal process, and his friendship, advice and kindness were much appreciated by surprisingly diverse people, as they had been in the internment camps and the ditches of the Pioneer Corps days. Although he felt himself old at Digswell, he was never short of friends or invitations for a drink or a meal. Hans was himself not inhospitable, though his way of life was frugal. Each month he received a parcel of excellent coffee sent by Lucie from the coffee shop by Albion Mews. His children visited him occasionally

with Francesca. Jane, who lived in his old flat in London, visited often, and on one occasion Bernard and Janet Leach came to Digswell, brought by Lucie. Janet Leach, whose Texan eyes could immediately see the power and importance of Hans's work, persuaded Bernard to buy her a pot by Hans, and by this means one of Hans's best known pots sat for many years in the window of Bernard Leach's St Ives flat, between him and the sea.

The visitors Hans most dreaded were the bailiffs, and he told Donald and Phyllis Brook that his home was deliberately sparsely furnished so that the bailiffs would have to go away empty-handed, since they were obliged to leave him one chair, one bed, one knife, one fork, one plate, and this was all he had. Fortuna-

tely they never came, but the financial pressures must have been very strong, and one available option was to teach.

Lucie Rie had agreed to teach students at the Camberwell School in London, when Bernard Leach and his son-in-law Dick Kendall, who was in charge of ceramics at Camberwell, convinced her that to pass on some of her experience was almost a duty. Lucie encouraged Hans to join her, and in 1961 he started as an associate lecturer, commuting one day a week from Digswell. On his first day he must have looked rather bewildered, or at least unsure of himself, to a tall young student who took Hans for a new recruit and assiduously showed him around, pointing out that this was a glazing room, this a kiln room, and just what a kiln was and did. The young man was Ian Godfrey, who had long admired Hans's pots but presumably had never seen his face.

It is true that Hans was diffident about his teaching abilities. He would go over and over his inadequacies as a teacher with Donald Brook in the long sessions at Digswell, and he genuinely believed a teacher needs training for the vocation, and that teaching *is* a vocation: those who did not feel the call should keep out. In later years, in correspondence with Donald, he would talk about his 'humbug', meaning his teaching activities. The irony is that Hans quickly became an exceptionally good teacher, out-teaching all his colleagues by his special ability to understand his students as individuals, and to teach them from within themselves.

Hans came to Camberwell with a specific brief – to teach architectural ceramics, the fruit of his experiences with the acoustic bricks and washbasins at Digswell. It was the early days of the art diploma called the 'Dip A.D.' and Hans's architectural course was just the sort of radical development the organisers liked. For Hans it was an opportunity to put into practice basic Bauhaus principles, and to get students to look for reasons rather than for solutions, to avoid style and panache and to seek essence. Hans's best known teaching tenet, *Why before How*, was probably coined at this period, and students of the time included John Minshall, Ewan Henderson and Anthony Hepburn, all of whom noted the impact that Hans's teaching made on the school, and on themselves. Hans, however, tired of the architectural course at about the same time as he became disillusioned with his industrial work, and he reverted to more direct tutorial teaching after two years.

For the financial security it gave him, Hans continued to teach for more than a decade, never taking his teaching duties lightly. He avoided promoting or even describing his own working methods, and concentrated instead on getting to know his students. In later years he regarded it as one of the benefits of teaching that it brought him into contact with people he liked. David Queensberry describes his teaching style in an illuminating way, and this is related in the next chapter.

By 1963 the initial group of artists at Digswell had begun to drift away. Donald Brook had left for Australia, Peter Collingwood went to Essex, Ralph Brown and John Wragg went towards the West Country. It had been a very stimulating group, with a good deal of dissent and argument and disharmony. Hans had managed to stay quietly on the outside, for he hated argument, but he must have been sad when good friends left. Then something came up for him: a small terraced house in West London, in a street condemned to demolition to make way for a new road, was offered at a low price. Lucie Rie, who had greatly missed Hans's daily presence in Albion Mews, was delighted to help Hans to buy the house, and in Spring 1963 Hans moved most of his things out of Digswell and back to London.

5
Princedale Road & Hammersmith

'I am an asphalt plant . . . What a relief to be back in London,' Hans wrote to Donald Brook, and mentioned an orgy of cinema-going. Though he kept options open by hanging on to the Digswell workshop for a time, the centre of gravity of Hans's life had moved back to town when he moved into No. 44 Princedale Road, West Kensington. It did not only provide him with a home and studio in one, but also represented a new personal commitment to sharing his life with Jane Gate and her two young sons, and from 1963 Hans and Jane remained together until Hans's death. One special feature of their relationship was the mutual respect each held for the other as an artist with a private right to work which must not be invaded.

The house was long and thin, extending from Princedale Road at the front to Pottery Lane at the back, where Hans had his studio and installed one of his two kilns. His work at the time included massive pots which had to be fired in pieces and assembled afterwards, and there were some architectural commissions. He was asked to make another ceramic mural for the boardroom of an advertising agency – another series of interlocking discs like those at Powell Duffryn House. The commission was done twice because of technical problems, and was finally installed with much approval and applause, until the arrival of the American art director. 'Elephants' arseholes . . .', and down came the discs. Hans got paid, but it was the last architectural commission he undertook. A large architectural mural for the Royal Army Pay Corps had been started and completed to Hans's satisfaction at Digswell, but it was still not up by the time he returned to London because the new building for which it was designed was still unfinished, and in due course Hans was called to help to erect it. Designing a ceramic version of a regimental cap badge made up of a lion and a crown is the sort of commission many different potters would tackle in many different ways. Knowing

Large pot outside Hans's London home.

that it was to be ten feet high, Hans broke the design down into handleable units and simplified the heraldic device to a basic but undistorted form, with the result that the lion mounted on an outside wall of the Armstrong Hall, Worthy Down, looks over the Hampshire landscape with the serene clarity of a neolithic white horse. It is shown here, together with the photograph Jane took of the lion in pieces on the Digswell floor.

It is extraordinary how many of the best known shapes developed by Hans had their beginnings in the Digswell workshop. Standing in the background of photographs taken for other purposes can often be seen shapes on shelves and in corners which had been thought to date from a later time. Perhaps this was because the London years from 1963 to 1967 were the most fertile years in terms of quantity of pots produced

Badge of the Royal Army Pay Corps, redesigned by Hans as a ceramic low relief, shown left in his studio, and above, mounted outside the Armstrong Hall, Worthy Down, Hampshire.

and the fuller development of certain shapes. After a period of settling in, during which he complained to Donald Brook that he could not get started, Hans began to make a series of large standing forms and to develop to perfection the onion shape which is probably world-wide the one form most closely associated with the name Coper. The Digswell pots tended to be jagged and metallic, with hard, often straight elements in the profile, shapes which could be mistaken for functional pieces of machinery, especially as the forms in question were almost always blackened with manganese. In London Hans turned again to rounded forms, and apart from the onions made many globular pots with flat discs on the top of, or below the globular shape — just above a stem — so that flatness and roundness are in counterpoint. In some large, spherical, bell-like forms the horizontal disc is only hinted at in the pro-file by means of an emergent belt, as if the pot is still spinning and the disc is in there trying to get out, like Saturn's rings.

The relationship of 'principal' form to its stand, stem or support was an intriguing aesthetic problem which he pursued for the rest of his life, and likewise the combination of a flattened rectilinear 'envelope' shape with a sphere, a form so closely associated with the London time that it has to be the symbol shape of this chapter (see page 61). Hans spent the London years refining and developing these shapes, and the London pots seem to be saying something very straightforward about gravity, whereas the pots of the later years are by contrast defying it. In this context it is an interest-ing exercise to look at some of the early pots upside down and see how they presage the forms at the end of the book.

After a year in Princedale Road, Hans moved his studio to a spacious garden shed in nearby Hammer-smith, bringing down the second kiln from Digswell. Jane's uncle's house by the river had two large out-buildings and one was used by Jane for photographic work, and the other was given to Hans. It was at this time that I myself first met Hans, in connection with a book I was preparing on modern ceramics, and I re-member well the special tranquil character of the Ham-mersmith studio, although it was very full of pots and only a few yards from the massive flow of traffic on the Great West Road. Thousands of motorists densely confined on this six-lane highway would find it hard to believe that, in the 1960s, there was a nest of studios and a variety of creative work in progress opposite Hammersmith's magnificent Edwardian town hall. Through a small door in the long, bland brick wall that fronts the road, Hans would go – like a vole to its hole in the riverbank – as the traffic swirled past, and when I asked him if the traffic was not an irritating distraction he said no, it was like the soothing sound of the sea.

To help my research, Hans told me exactly how he went about making the various composite forms he had developed. Without the explanation he gave, it would be difficult now to say for certain exactly what the sequence was, for even Lucie is hesitant about say-ing how some of the forms were made. Clearly many of the large pots are far too big to have been thrown in one piece, and Hans used the traditional method of add-ing a coil on top of a thrown form when it had strength-ened by drying, and throwing on up, several times

Pots in the making in the Hammersmith studio. Most of those shown above were exhibited in the Berkeley Gallery in 1965.

Cup form thrown in two pieces, with flange thrown from an added coil. Coated in manganese dioxide, 14 cm high, 1965. Collection of J. W. N. van Achterbergh.

if necessary, till he reached the required height. The horizontal flanges such as are shown on pages 123 and 128 were also thrown from coils after the main form had hardened, as in the case of the cup forms shown left and the spherical and bottle forms on pages 132–5. The precisely level top of these pots is essential to their character, and is easier to achieve with the 'new' clay from a coil than the tired clay pulled out from the top of a form just thrown.

The onion shapes on pages 125–7 are made in two thrown pieces, joined at the narrowest part, just as were the 'metallic' Digswell forms on pages 111 and 114. The massive bowls and bells, page 105 and right, are made in two pieces and joined in the middle. For Hans there was no interest in the special prowess of throwing something difficult. If it was easier and more efficient to make two small forms and then join them, he would do this to achieve the end product that he held in his mind. In this respect he showed an engineer's regard for structures and mechanics, taking the shortest cut to achieve the economy of form compatible with function, like a modern bridge designer. Virtuosity in itself, which quite reasonably sustains many potters, was not for him.

In other potters' workshops strange-shaped pots sometimes appear in which the form is the result of the potter taking action (often accidental in the first place) in distorting the form. Although such pots can be quite dynamic, they are always slight or transient. Hans's unusual forms were never achieved in this way. He created the form in his mind and then found a technique that would realise it. He often drew the pots he was going to make in chalk or pencil or clay, on anything that was handy, and I can well remember how practically every flat surface in the Hammersmith studio had prototype pots drawn out in firm outline. Some of these drawings can be seen near the base of the pot on page 61.

The joining together of separately thrown items can be clumsy or inharmonious. Some of the rather pudgy thistle forms of Albion Mews days seem to be untidy where the joins are made, but by the Hammersmith period these joins were clean and did not jar. The insides of all the pots were coated with manganese, sometimes with a clear glaze over to ensure that they would be waterproof and could be used as containers for flowers. Manganese and the glaze would be poured into the pot – the only way of getting at the surface – and the surplus poured off when the inside was coated. The outside surface of a pot like that shown here is created as follows. After throwing, and when the pot has become nearly dry, deep scratches running diagonally are made in the surface with a serrated metal tool known as a sculptor's riffler. The manganese and iron mixture is then painted on with a brush, all over, and this dries immediately. By sanding with fine sandpaper and rubbing down, white clay is exposed, leaving dark manganese in the scratches. The surface is then painted with a white slip made from feldspar, china clay and whiting, and when dry it is sanded again, so that most of the slip is removed. More slip is then painted on, thickly round the base, and the brush marks are allowed to show. Near the top of the pot it is banded with manganese (i.e. the manganese is painted on when the pot is revolving), and this application may be made with a brush or a sponge. The process of coating alternately with manganese and slip is often repeated several times. Only when the surface is precisely as required is the pot fired, once. But that is not the end of the process, for the fired pot comes somewhat sulkily out of the kiln, and to acquire its luminescence and rich patina it is thoroughly burnished, in the case of black pots using an emery wheel attached to an electric drill. Hans's pots are always coloured or 'slipped' right down to the base, and the base itself is carefully ground so that it will not scratch. Finally, to make sure it is functional, Johnson's furniture wax is added to the inside with the pot still hot from the kiln, so that water cannot seep through the open-textured clay.

Hans's most recent exhibition in the Berkeley Galleries had been a shared exhibition with Lucie in 1956, and William Ohly invited Hans to hold a one-man show there in October 1965. In preparation for this, families of pots multiplied on the slatted shelves of the Hammersmith studio, and the large exhibition carefully arranged by Hans himself was a great success. Hans described it in a letter to Donald Brook as 'a shot in the arm', shortly to be followed by participation in a good exhibition at the Molton Gallery in South Molton Street called 'The Potter's World', and organised and selected by Edwin Mullins.

Although Hans was participating in London and provincial exhibitions he had a fairly jaundiced view about the art world. He expressed this privately to Donald Brook:

> The general race is increasing in momentum. There is so much going on. The Art Schools are turning out geniuses. Art is an overcrowded profession,

Large bell form made in Hammersmith in 1965, 48 cm high.

A range of shapes in a corner of the Hammersmith workshop, 1965.

more than when you left. Although I am almost completely out of touch, I cannot help noticing that this is becoming the Art Age. Not so long ago you had to look for it, now it is all over the place, and the Royal College seems to have the monopoly.

He goes on to explain how he had been offered a well paid job with light teaching duties at the University of Chicago (a job which was later taken by Ruth Duckworth) but had turned it down because he could not face the thought of being on show on an American campus. However, in April 1966, in another letter to Donald Brook, he said:

> I seem to get more and more involved with teaching. The latest is – you may laugh by all means – a day a week at the Royal College from September . . . I was also offered a senior lectureship at Camberwell, but having been there now for some time I realised that this would be a fate worse than death, shut my eyes to the money, and declined. The truth is I am not in the least blasé about being offered these jobs, but that I rather despise myself for having to accept them. You know my peculiar attitude to what I do.

Coming to terms with absurdity privately is one thing, and I am pretty good at it by now, but being appointed to do it institution-wise is often as demoralising as I had always thought it could not fail to be.

Hans clearly felt he had some explaining to do in revealing that he was now adding his weight and support to the Royal College of Art. His increasing reputation and his accessibility in London now meant that he was in great demand as a teacher and as an examiner. In the busy year of 1966 he was invited to give a day's seminar at the Harrow School of Art, where a workmanlike practical pottery course, shaped by Victor Margrie and Mick Casson, was in full swing. Aware that this course was thought by some people to be short on aesthetics, the organisers were delighted when Hans agreed to come. It turned out to be rather a strange day, which started, to Hans's surprise, with a showing of the film about the country potter Isaac Button. 'Here is a real potter,' said Hans, 'Why do you want me?' Such genuine modesty confounded and confused everyone, and Hans proceeded to destroy more illusions by talking about his understanding of 'repeat work'. 'He was supposed to be the one-off sculptural potter,' said a student, 'and here he was talking about "one kick of the wheel, one saucer".' Hans's years in Albion Mews making tea sets had been overlooked; he had experienced what these young men and women were being trained for, and he disarmed his audience in their own defensive stance. He refused the absurd task of teaching aesthetics to the students at Harrow, nor did he want to describe his own techniques; instead he told them about his days in the quiet corridors of the British Museum, looking at Egyptian, Mycenean and Cycladic sculpture.

The atmosphere softened when they all retired to Lyons Tea Shop and talked about jazz, and Hans agreed that improvisation around a theme was part of his own pottery. I am not convinced that Hans was being serious here. It was more likely to have been his way of finding a common topic of interest as the starting point for serious talk.

It was in one-to-one tutorial teaching that Hans was most at ease and most appreciated, and when he went to the Royal College there began a period which has been described by all concerned as memorable and never repeated.

Hans continued to teach there as a once-a-week visitor until 1975. David Queensberry, then professor at the Royal College of Art, persuaded Hans to take on the job, and much later wrote in *Crafts Magazine*, 'This is the most important thing that I have done in twenty years work at the College.' He believed that Hans had more influence in his years there than any other teacher since Staite Murray, and the students, had they known Staite Murray, would probably have been of the same mind. They certainly all remember the extraordinary impact of Hans as a teacher: gentle yet shattering. He had an amazing ability to get inside the mind of the student, to become a critic from within the person. He was in no way dogmatic, and would question not what they were doing, but why. *Why before How* ruthlessly stripped away the pretentiousness that an art school environment can encourage, and Hans would gently redirect his students to face themselves as their own prime critics. But it was Hans's respect for the dignity of all people – even the rawest student – that made him so much loved by a whole generation of students at the College, for he would never deliberately set about destroying the ego of his students – he simply encouraged them to think things out for themselves and to keep their standards high. As a result his students often felt that everything they were making was being made for Hans. Alison Britton, writing of Hans's influence, said, 'I felt an urgent need to have something better to show him the next time he came,' and Elizabeth Fritsch, who was also taught by him in the 1960s, wrote, 'His teaching had the same integrity and strength as had his pots; graceful, direct, precisely and sensitively tuned. . . .'

Graceful is a rather emotive and somewhat surprising word to describe both Hans's pots and his person, but it is most appropriate. It related to his politeness, and his way of conducting all human relationships. In personal relationships there was always dignity, and his pots both command and *offer* respect. Hans's concern regarding his ineffectiveness as a teacher was not well founded.

The year in which the Royal College teaching began saw a new period of cooperation with Lucie Rie, this time with a major joint exhibition in Europe, to be shown first at the Boymans Museum in Rotterdam from April to June 1967, and then moving on to Arnhem. Working flat out at the Hammersmith studios Hans produced his share of the 360 pots which were taken to Holland early in that year. The organiser of the exhibition, Miss Bernardine de Neeve, put the modern central galleries of the Boymans Museum at the disposal of Hans and Lucie, and the appearance

of the exhibition can be seen from the photograph overleaf.

By now Hans was very wary of any words used to describe his work, and in the introduction by Douglas Hill to the Dutch exhibition a major effort was made,

Two large pots with spherical bases stand on a wooden turntable covered with drawings of pottery forms.

Coper pots at the Boymans exhibition, Rotterdam, 1967.

with Hans's cooperation, to put his philosophy of pot-making into words:

> In Coper's work, one can see not so much a quality of serenity as a kind of balanced tension. Coper seems to be exploring the outward limits of pottery, and to be pushing those limits back with each new motif. Yet never (and from here the tension arises) does he lose sight of the true nature of pottery. He never sculpts; he makes pots. In the process he is enlarging his own concept, and ours, of the essential 'potness' of a pot.

There had never been any question in Hans's mind of mixing up pottery and sculpture – indeed he would have shuddered at the current practice in museums of describing his work as 'pot-sculptures' – but having left sculpture behind entirely, he had to define his position. All his works were containers dependent upon ceramic techniques, thrown on a wheel. In this context it is important to point out that part of their energy comes from the fact that they are made on the wheel. The impact of such forms as those shown on page 113 *depends* on the wheel. Indeed they could not have been conceived without it.

In Spring 1967, in preparation for this most prestigious exhibition of his career to date, Hans applied for a passport. With Lucie he went to Holland before the opening to check on preparations, and then went to Holland again, this time with his children Anya and Laurens, for the opening itself. Anya was by now an adult and Laurens was leaving school days behind. Both had had to grow up with only occasional contact with their father, and the expedition to Rotterdam was a marvellous experience for both generations. Hans was able to contact a German uncle and a cousin who had been living in Holland since the war, and the children went on holiday abroad with their father for the first time. The excitement was enormous, especially when they found that their father was famous. It was a formal occasion, and Hans was surprised and embarrassed to find himself so much in the limelight.

Almost all the pots which went to Holland were sold there, but one particular sale gave Hans special pleasure. The men of the museum who had built the stand and arranged the pots were seeking a wedding present for a colleague. They clubbed together and bought one of the Copers.

6 Frome

Hans was taken by Jane in early 1967 to a derelict farm and empty farmhouse for sale in a valley near Frome in Somerset, and his comment was positive enough: 'No! Never! All those roofs!' But the urge to move to the country was strong in both of them, and they had the means to buy it. Ironically it was not the success of Hans's pottery which gave him for the first time in his life some cash in his pocket, but the lifting of the threat of road building in London. The Princedale Road house doubled in value overnight, and Hans and Jane were able to buy the little farm, and had the money to create a studio alongside. Thus the 'asphalt plant', whose lifestyle had been austere and who had ignored personal possessions, rather shamefacedly wrote to Donald Brook in Australia that he was 'a man of property'. The move to Frome in 1967 was the beginning of the final phase in Hans's life – the most tranquil period, one of the most productive, and the longest, for Hans and Jane lived together at Spring Gardens, Frome, for fourteen years.

It was Autumn 1967 before they could move in, with minimal but very necessary building work to be done, and the studio to be converted from a barn. Camping in a house without the electricity connected, he wrote again to Donald Brook, 'We have a lot of plums on the premises – the only life we found in this derelict place – Jane has dried some and they are like walnuts, we also have a walnut tree – I suspect it will produce plums. And we have a hedge of flowering lettuce for a windbreak.' One of the first things to do was to put a damp course into the house, and Hans decided to try out a new chemical method, which meant the insertion of hygroscopic rods into the masonry of the house. Holes had to be drilled through the walls all round the house, two inches apart, just above ground level, and I remember Hans saying he had turned the house into a piece of lavatory paper, ready to be torn away along the perforations by the wind. The house itself was not very old – eighteenth century – with the high-pitched roof typical of Frome, and there were a good many limestone walls round the property in various stages of dilapidation. Building the studio meant reroofing and glazing the high barn next to the cowshed, with the concreting of floors and the rebuilding of the gable wall. In what appeared to be a very short time everything was organised. A new, large electric kiln was installed and also a tortoise stove, Hans himself making the pottery cowl to fit where the flue from the stove emerged from the roof.

Jane felt that their lives in London were constantly being interrupted by visitors, and their flight to the country would provide them with an uninterrupted opportunity for new work. For Jane, leaving a professional career as a photographer behind, the change

Hans back in the country, and, opposite, the farm at Spring Gardens as it was in 1967.

was total and dramatic, although she was really only returning to a rural lifestyle she had known in her childhood. Weaving, gardening and, later on, goats occupied her time and attention. For Hans there was no change in activity – the families of pots started to flow from his wheel as soon as the workshop was operational, but he had a real townsman's feel for the countryside and nature – a more observant eye for clouds, trees in bud, birds and rural forms than many a farmer's boy or country parson's son. For Hans, time off in earlier years had always meant time in the country, by the sea looking for fossils, at monuments like Stonehenge, or merely walking through the Autumn leaves on Hampstead Heath. He did not visit cities or spectacular places, and apart from the two short trips already mentioned to Paris and Rotterdam he never went abroad. One contemporary artist with whom he had a great sympathy and similarity was Giacometti, and Giacometti (who had died in 1966) was able to put into words exactly how Hans felt about many things, including the reasons why he had no need to travel. Speaking in Paris, Giacometti said:

> The tree on a Paris pavement is already enough. One tree is enough for me. The thought of seeing two was frightening. Where I used to want to travel, these days it makes no difference whether I do or not. The curiosity to see things lessens, because a glass on a table astounds me much more than before.
>
> If the glass there in front of me astounds me more than all the glasses that I have seen in paintings, and if I even think that the greatest wonder of wonders in world architecture couldn't affect me more than the glass, it's not really worthwhile going to the Indies to see some temple or other when I have as much and more right in front of me.

Hans was not a figurative artist like Giacometti, but in the return again and again to a single theme in the search for essence by reduction and simplification, and the refusal ever to consider the possibility of being satisfied with any result, the two men have much in common. This common ground extends to their work: like Giacometti's figures, Hans's work is timeless, with roots in the far past and in anonymous or folk art, yet it also belongs to its own time and contains the rolled-up experience of the twentieth century.

No sooner had Hans made his workshop ready than he was engaged every working hour in another major exhibition. His old Digswell colleague Peter Collingwood had been asked by the Victoria & Albert Museum in London if he would like to mount an exhibition of his weavings. The suggestion came from Hugh Wakefield, of the museum's Circulation Department, and this was soon followed by a second suggestion: 'Would you like to share your exhibition with a potter?' Collingwood had misgivings, but these turned to delight when he heard the potter in question might be Hans. The two men got together again and decided that the show should not be retrospective, as had been envisaged – after all, both were in mid career and under fifty years old – and so everything was made especially for the exhibition within the twelve months that preceded its opening in January 1969. The Victoria & Albert invited an architect, Alan Irvine, to design the exhibition on a very low budget, and Hans in particular was disappointed that he would not

be in charge of the design himself.

Although it was an important event and finally established Hans – in the words of his admiring friend Jupp Dernbach – 'in the prime position of all potters', the relations between the museum and the artists were not altogether happy. The Victoria & Albert has, under new direction, become much more commercially orientated since 1969, but at the time the organisers felt that to sell work on display was rather beneath their dignity. The artists got the impression that the work could be for sale, yes, provided no one knew about it. For both men to have been encouraged to work at full stretch for a year, thus reducing their earning capacity to nil, and then for no effort to be made to sell their work was very irritating, and the artists threatened to remove their work unless a price list was displayed.

Hans made a massive number of pots and finally allowed well over a hundred into the exhibition, all of which were photographed for Hans by Jane, several of the pictures appearing in this book (see pages 154–8, and 160). The pots were in series, or families, comprising a dozen basic shapes. Most of them were a refinement of shapes already produced at Digswell or Hammersmith, but making their first public appearance were the attenuated pots on bases which were to preoccupy Hans so much in his Frome years, and which are often called the 'Cycladic' pots.

Hans had at one time tried to overcome the practical difficulties of making a swelling form stable when rising from a tiny base by crowding and sticking several pots together so that, in contact, they would help to support one another as tripods (see page 101), but the inevitable grouping of the pots somehow ran counter to the spirit of Hans's work, and they seemed relatively trivial in comparison to those which concentrate the attention rather than dividing it.

As an alternative method he developed the practice of mounting a shape (consisting often of two interlocking forms) on a small drum-like thrown base, by drilling the two parts and cementing them together on a piece of steel knitting needle. This allowed the point of contact between pot and base to be reduced to two or three millimetres without any loss of strength. The forms remained containers, unlike the totemic Cycladic figures with which they were identified, and they were designed to stand rather than to be held in the hand. The association with Cycladic art does not have to be pursued too far. It is a convenient label for a distinctive batch of work, and that Hans, like Giacometti and Brancusi, loved Cycladic carving with its

Collingwood wall hangings and Coper pots in the Victoria & Albert exhibition, 1969.

dense energy and sexuality was beyond question, but Hans's progress in developing these small, late pots was an inventive one. He was not copying or even working parallel to the Cycladic figures; he was still making pots. To talk, therefore, of 'sexual imagery' in Hans Coper's pots was meaningless. Sex is part of all of them, from the very beginning of his career, and this is true of most pottery anyway. It became more marked, especially in work made at Frome as Hans grew more remote from the functional pottery of the Albion Mews days.

After the intense period of work for the Victoria & Albert Museum exhibition, Hans turned his attention for a time elsewhere – to architecture. The farmhouse at Spring Gardens was quite large, even allowing for rooms for visitors and a self-contained section carpentered by Hans for his daughter Anya, who came to live there for a time. It was not, therefore, strictly from necessity that new living quarters were designed by Hans and built at right angles to the main house, pointing towards his studio amongst the outbuildings. I believe that Hans simply wanted to design a house from scratch, as many a would-be architect has done before him, and in this account of Hans and his pottery it might seem worth only a passing mention, had the design not been so very good.

He tackled the challenge of adding something new to an eighteenth-century building head-on, using concrete blocks and float-finished cement, wired glass where necessary, exposed joists and a unique fully glazed gable wall. The result is a tidy design, efficient in space and in heating, and with its steep pitched roof in total harmony with the farmhouse at its side. The new building, which became Jane's own living quarters, is a remarkable one, and can be seen below and on the right. It has no luxury and no decoration. The floor is bare concrete, and most of the surfaces are untreated, left as they were installed by the builder. It has, though, no lack of comfort and generates a sense of well-being and light, and Hans tackled every detail with fresh and unfatigued eyes. Apart from having doors and windows, walls and a staircase, it has absolutely nothing in common with any other house built in Frome in 1969. Mr Cray, Hans's local builder, called Hans a perfectionist.

The main living room and, right, the exterior of Hans's extension to the farm at Spring Gardens.

Hans's wartime friend Howard Mason the architect was still a close companion. He was able to come to Frome easily from his Cheltenham home, and thoroughly appreciated the new building, which he studied in great detail down to its thoughtful door handles. He called it 'basic', which was high praise. Hans must have been very pleased by this reaction, for Howard's good opinion was something he valued in exactly the way in which most people valued Hans's. Howard Mason was still his mentor: when making pots Hans would ask himself, 'Would this be good enough for Howard?'

The first five or six years at Frome were happy ones. The deep depressions which had pursued him to Digswell and in London did not return. What did continue, however, were the occasional, but rather prolonged, periods in which he did no apparent work. It was as if he were taking long gulps of air from the door of his studio before diving back inside, fortified for the next confrontation with the clay. There was no self-satisfied relaxation involved in these workless periods, for work and the inevitability of his return to it sooner or later was a rule by which he lived. Work was an unconventional form of religion to him. Uninterested in the formal trappings of any kind of church, he was not an aggressively Godless person, and in fact found hearty atheism in some ways an affront to the dignity of life. It is Jane's belief that Hans worked as an offering to an undefined deity, and many people find the pots he produced intensely spiritual. It has been said that such pots could not have been made by a man with no religion. They are not apeing votive objects of Classical or pre-Classical time; they are themselves an offering from the twentieth century, and made by a man far from indifferent to the goings-on of the present day and who brought Hiroshima and all unnecessary modern suffering into his work. It is precisely because his range of interests and concern was so wide that his pots are so moving.

Frome is not far from North Curry, where the old

Takoma School was based, and only a few miles from Bruton where an ex-Takoma colleague, Henk Huffener, had established an informal art centre in a converted chapel. Hans was pleased to meet Henk again, and he often visited the Bruton centre where he was introduced to other artists, including Ernst Blensdorf. Blensdorf, like Hans, had fled from Germany, but not as a youth; he was a professor of Fine Arts whose work and views did not suit the Nazi regime. He set up a studio for his wood carving in Bruton, where Hans met him as an old man, and admired his work which was in the style of Barlach. The Copers made many new friends in Somerset, but the peace and quiet of the countryside they thought they had found in Spring Gardens was often broken by old friends visiting, and there was a great deal of laughter and merriment, especially over long, long lunches, with a lot of beer drunk. 'We laughed so much it almost seemed wicked,' said Jane. 'It was not all work. . . .'

In 1970 there were many exhibitions, including Expo 1970 in Osaka, the Museum of Modern Art in Kyoto, and a commercial gallery exhibition in Tokyo. Hans contributed work to all three Japanese exhibitions as well as a travelling exhibition in America and a mixed exhibition in Copenhagen. It was at Nottingham, however, that he had a one-man show at the Midland Group Gallery in this year, and this was much admired. In a 'good year' Hans would make as many

Lucie Rie was a regular visitor to Hans's home in Frome.

In the carefully arranged one-man show Hans held at the Midland Group, Nottingham, in 1970, the considerable variation in scale within the families of pots is clearly seen.

as two hundred pots, and the years from 1968 to 1972 were all very productive ones. Throughout this time he was continuing to teach at the Royal College, although he had given up the Camberwell visiting-lectureship when he moved to Frome. Driving to London and back to Frome meant getting up at 5 a.m. and coming home at about 10 p.m. in the evening. He would sometimes, when working through a large batch of pots, go straight into the studio after the journey and work on into the night, though he confided to his students that his one day a week in London took about three days of energy, and it was a great physical strain. The Royal College teaching was an important source of income, and as well as bringing him into contact with students whom he liked, he was able to meet Lucie regularly, and would call for breakfast, lunch and often dinner on his college days before setting off for home. Lucie herself was one of the most regular of all visitors to Frome, and another surprising guest there was Walter Coper, back in Europe from South America. Walter had been to England more than once since his 1960 visit, and the relationship between the brothers grew stronger with each trip. By the early 1970s, however, as a result of the political persecution

in Chile following the overthrow of the Allende regime, Walter had gone back to Germany to live and work in Berlin, and so his visits to England were more regular.

Hans could never be persuaded to return to Germany, and when in 1972 a joint retrospective exhibition was held in Hamburg for Hans and Lucie, organised by Dr Spielmann at the Museum für Kunst und Gewerbe, neither potter was there for the opening. It is ironic that, of all countries it was Germany, which Hans had found so threatening, that was most respectful towards him and eager for his work.

In the early 1970s Hans worked for and exhibited in Henry Rothschild's annual pottery collection in the Cambridge centre known as Kettle's Yard, and in the Summer of 1972 the International Ceramics Exhibition of the Academy of Ceramics based in Geneva came to London. Hans was one of the selectors for the British exhibit. His standards were rigorous throughout, and he found himself in the embarrassing position of having rejected all the work submitted by the rest of the selection committee. It was the last time that Hans accepted such a task, and soon he was to give up teaching too. As early as 1974 there were signs of a deterioration in his physical co-ordination. The stiffening of his spine had been held at bay through treatment, and he had some relief from pain through drugs. However, he started to have difficulty in the use of his left leg, and friends and neighbours in Frome noticed a clumsiness in carrying everyday objects and some hesitancy in walking. By 1975 Hans was really markedly changing, and he was having difficulty with his speech.

Robert Welch, the silversmith and industrial designer with a workshop in Chipping Camden, asked Hans if he would like to exhibit in the small gallery there, usually used for paintings and sculpture. Hans prepared a collection of thirty recent pots, including about ten of his newly evolved Cycladic forms, as illustrated on pages 194–7. In this breathtaking collection Hans seems to have carried to the ultimate the purity of form he had been seeking for so long. The new pots, though small, seem to concentrate energy and to be denser than anything natural. Hans had pursued Mies van de Rohe's maxim, *Less means More* and produced his finest forms. The white pots were whiter, the surface more luminescent; the black pots were blacker, but burnished to a graphite-like sheen. A relatively new surface texture was on view in which the white slip was encouraged to flake away, leaving an orangey-red base clay showing through. The pots were

Robert Welch Gallery, Chipping Camden, 1975.

delivered to Chipping Camden by Hans himself in August. Although Copers were being shown more and more abroad, especially in Germany, it was five years since a major collection had been seen in England, and visitors came long distances to visit the tiny gallery in the Cotswolds. The prices were relatively high, but the response to the work was unanimous. Reviewers were enthusiastic about shapes which had never before been exhibited.

Hans was too ill to go to the opening, and was now undergoing tests in connection with his increasing difficulty with speaking, walking and using his left hand. Motor-neurone disease, or amyotrophic lateral sclerosis (ALS) was diagnosed in 1975. His doctor explained to him as much as was known of this illness; it is a relatively rare disease, with outward manifestations similar to those of a stroke. The degeneration of motor-neurones in the cortex of the brain, and their fibre tracts, produces a slowly developing paralysis. There is no known cause, and no cure.

Hans had confided in the Brooks at Digswell that he most feared a general seizing-up of his body following the stiffening of his upper spine in the 1950s, and he had to face in 1975 a future of increasing immobility. News of his illness filtered through to all those connected with ceramics, and it was widely rumoured that Hans was suffering from manganese poisoning, an occupational hazard for those who worked with the element. In Hans's case this was a plausible assumption, since manganese dioxide was the one metal oxide

that Hans used constantly. It is important for other potters who spend much time with the material to know that Hans's illness had nothing to do with manganese, or with any other metals, and that it is very unlikely that there is any connection between pottery-making and ALS.

From 1975 onwards, Hans had to make progressive adjustments to his way of life, and spend more of his time in his studio, less in the open. His nearest neighbours, Ted and Doreen Appleby, who had helped Jane with her weaving and her goats and were frequent visitors to the house, saw Hans still throwing with apparent ease after his illness started, but he shook his head and said, 'You should have seen me in my heyday.' Hans responded to certain commissions and made pots specially for visiting clients.

He continued to make the Cycladic pots until the shelves in the small studio adjoining his main workshop were filled with pots so compelling that the visual din was too much to bear, and Hans had special roller blinds made to hide his own work from view. He rarely left the precincts of the house and workshop after 1975, though one day the Applebys drove Jane and Hans on an outing that was particularly memorable. They went to Avebury, not far from Frome, where the great neolithic stone circle and the artefacts found nearby had so much impressed and influenced Lucie Rie on a visit during the war. Hans had never been before, and was impressed, not just by the prehistory but by the whole atmosphere and architecture of the village, and he promised to return. It was difficult, however, for him to be mobile and he was having increasing difficulty in making himself understood. Amyotrophic lateral sclerosis affects the muscles of the throat and tongue, and distorts speech. It leaves the intellect unimpaired.

From 1976 he spent all his daytime hours in his studio. Jane looked after him and spent as much time with him as he wanted, but he was usually alone, as he had been when working at full stretch. Apart from Lucie, whose company was always welcome, not many other visitors stayed very long, since it was a strain for him to talk and hard work for him to listen. Some of the most ardent collectors of his work who visited him and were welcome at this time were from Germany, and these included Paul Köster from Mönchengladbach, Rainer Klinge from Hanover, and Harald Muhlhausen from Darmstadt. It was not the presence of a man in pain and in poor health which was so moving to Harald Muhlhausen, it was the fact that Hans was so warm and

25 Dec 75

Dear Mr. Mühlehausen,

For your kind letter and good wishes many thanks.

Work now goes very slowly and I produce little. I will certainly keep your preference in mind & still hope to have at least a few things to show you on your next visit — to which we look forward.

With friendly greetings and our best wishes to you and Mrs. Mühlehausen from us both

Yours sincerely,

Hans Coper.

friendly, and himself took pleasure in the knowledge that his pots were an effective means of communication with people in all walks of life. For Harald Muhlhausen, knowing Hans was an enrichment of his life. They would talk of German wine and remembered experiences of German life, such as the 'blumchenkaffee' drunk by poor people in Germany, so thin that the flowers on the bottom of the cups could be seen through the liquid. Towards the end of his life Hans said to Muhlhausen that his pots were getting smaller and smaller, like Hans himself. A gentle, formal correspondence developed between the two men, from Hans's side neither particularly personal nor informative, but treasured by Harald in the same way that I treasure Hans's letters to me – because the handwriting is so beautiful. The fine, strong words stride across the paper, with Japanese-like calligraphy, and in spite of the progression of Hans's illness he was still writing beautifully in 1980. An early letter to Harald Muhlhausen had been written on Christmas Day 1975, and is shown here in full. It just fails to state the fact that Hans's career was now nearly complete.

When Giacometti, knocked down by a bus in Paris, was asked by someone, perhaps a reporter from *France-Culture*, 'What were your first thoughts ... ?' he said unhesitatingly, 'I thanked God that I would not have to make any more sculpture.' Hans likewise felt that his illness was a justifiable release from his contract as a potter. Although he had said to Jane that he would always find a way of working, he said pointedly to an old friend that 'people who paint with their feet paint very bad pictures.' By the time that his left hand had become immobile in 1978, he said, 'It doesn't matter – I cannot improve on what I have done. I have just about come to the end.'

After 1979 Hans made no new pots. He drew blinds down over the shelves on which he kept his best work, so that it could not be seen. For two years he spent most of his time alone, reading more and more, listening to music or writing in the notebook on his desk. The radio which had played constantly in his working days was supplemented with a television set, but a black and white one, for the colour set which came first was too confusing to his perceptions in general. 'I looked out of the window and wanted to turn the window off.' The window was his greatest interest, and with binoculars he would watch birds and everything in the garden outside. His daughter Anya remembers him sitting in the studio in darkness for many hours in the evenings. By 1980 Hans decided not to attempt to go

to the house, and the smaller studio was carefully redesigned into living quarters where he lived by choice alone. In his room he had time to study everything in front of him, and this included a mouse, and then a family of mice which provided him with company. He drew the mouse on the back of an envelope for Lucie – a mere cartoon, but his last drawing. In 1980 he had his last firing of pots, which had been assembled long before and with painful slowness prepared for the kiln. All the writing, which had occupied two years, he burned.

Pain-relieving drugs were prescribed, but the side effects they induced brought Hans little relief from pain and discomfort. His doctor believed that he had a determination, like Rilke whose works were by his bedside and who suffered a similar disease, to contain his own destiny and to experience pain and suffering and hopelessness, and thereby find a definition for such words that people use without knowing what they mean. It was not a masochistic exercise. It was part of a philosophy which formed Hans many years before: 'Endure your own destiny'. In 1981 he had difficulty in swallowing. By his bedside was a whisky bottle which contained just water. In June he contracted pneumonia, and he died on June 16th.

7 Epilogue

For Hans's sixtieth birthday on April 8th 1980 a special exhibition was mounted in his honour at the Hetjens Museum in Dusseldorf. The keeper, Dr Ekkart Klinge, had no difficulty in gathering together the forty exhibits entirely from private collectors in Germany and Holland and the work was all from the 1960s and '70s, including some of the last pots Hans made. It was obvious to Dr Klinge, who had recently met Hans in Frome, that this was to be a valedictory exhibition, and in the tribute he wrote in the accompanying catalogue he emphasised Hans's unique position in European ceramics as a creator of new forms and new values, affecting the way in which all ceramics would be judged. This was the last exhibition in Hans's lifetime, and collectors in particular realised that their opportunities of finding new work were shrinking away.

By 1980 the Fine Art auction houses had discovered the commercial potential in twentieth century ceramics, and pots by Leach and Hamada were fetching sums which really interested them. Hans's pots that he had sold for tens of pounds were being auctioned for hundreds, and in October 1980 at a sale at Sotheby's, Belgravia, an early 'thistle' pot realised nearly £8000. Since this was by far the highest sum ever paid for a work by a living potter, and was exceeded shortly afterwards in a private gallery sale of another Coper, Sotheby's jubilantly broadcast the event with the headline, 'Hans Up'. The hunt for Copers of all periods began, with prices henceforth always in four figures.

Hans was amused by the turn of events, though he must have found the irony of his late success, in his own phrase, 'quite idiotic'. For the pots were the same pots; only the wind had changed.

He did not like his work to be cupboarded away, and the thought of it out of sight or in bank vaults would have disappointed him. He liked his pots to be in the hands – if not literally, then certainly within touching distance – of people who responded to them, and both collectors and friends have remarked on the intense way in which he watched when a visitor was choosing a pot. It is natural that collectors of ceramics would want to have Copers in their collection, but it is interesting how so many people with no special interest in ceramics warmed to his pots and collected *only* Copers. It is also revealing how people who are not interested in collecting anything at all find his work rivetting, as if Hans had set some ultra-sonic music abroad, and to them a single pot is more than just an object. Alan Firth of Leeds, who first became aware of Hans Coper's work in the 1970s, is one such entrapped admirer, both of the work and of the man. He describes holding a Hans Coper pot in his hand as 'much more than a kind of balm' – it appeared to him to have a positive message to the intellect and to the senses.

When Hans was sure that he had communicated through his work in this way he was content, and if he felt it had some meaning he was most generous in giving pots to his friends. They received gifts of Hans's cherished work as a sort of reciprocal act of respect. As early as 1956 Ove Arup, when he was opening a Berkeley Gallery exhibition, said of Lucie and Hans together:

> They do not want to be considered as artists making collectors' pieces for connoisseurs and art critics . . . they want to establish that contact and understanding between the artist and his audience which is so essential to the thriving of Fine Art.

Like Lucie, Hans, by remaining true to himself, succeeded in this communication. Of this there is no doubt, and pots were his only means of saying what he wanted to say. In spite of his verbal dexterity and humour in conversation, he found the written word an agony, which is probably why he burned his own writings before he died. It is characteristic of him not to leave anything around which was not up to his own high standards. It is not widely known that he had serious misgivings about the short personal statement he wrote for the beginning of the Coper/Collingwood exhibition catalogue, and which is taken by many as a moving expression of his views. He found the written word too much of a commitment, and by paring words away he felt that what remained said either too little or too much. He disliked the fulsome and effusive in all things, just as he discarded the woolly and vague. He loved art that came from the head, and art that came from the heart, and in his works he exhibited both.

Jupp Dernbach said of him:

'He was so gifted, I cannot compare him with anyone else.'

Many of the photographs on the succeeding pages were taken by Jane Coper and others at the time of making, or before the pots were exhibited and sold. It is thus not possible in every instance to indicate present ownership.

One of a series of composite pots made by Hans in the early 1950s, comprising four thrown units, including two bowls joined face to face. Height: 44 cm.

Left: an early jug, c. 40 cm high, which may have been made before 1950. Hans left it behind at the Albion Mews pottery, but the surface clearly shows that he had already learned the technique for the vitreous white slip which characterised all his work for the next thirty years. Above: a black jug with white sgraffito design, c. 1952. This pot was more highly valued by Hans – he priced it at ten guineas. Height: 40 cm. Right: a black vase with white sgraffito design, photographed by Hans himself in 1950. Its height and whereabouts are unknown, but it is the earliest example of a vase with an emergent ring half way down the form.

Round pots, 1953. The dark pot is 21 cm diameter, sgraffito through manganese to bare white clay. The light pots have linear sgraffito through two coats of white slip to manganese under-painting. Pot at left: 32 cm diameter, pot at right: 29 cm diameter.

Left: two 'treacle' pots made in the early 1950s, top one 14 cm high, lower one 11 cm. Although recognisable as Coper shapes, these unique pots bear a shiny, iron-rich amber glaze. *Lucie Rie.*

Right: tall vase, 35 cm high, sgraffito to manganese under-painting through white slip. With its emphasis on the surface texture, this is a painter's pot. *c.* 1953. *Dr Youngman.*

Waisted vase, *c.* 1954, 31·5 cm high. In this beautiful pot the typical sgraffito is beginning to turn to the more regular scratched surface of later work.

Left: globular pot, 31 cm high. Gold medal in Milan Triennale 1953. Right: poppy-head pot, 30 cm high. A high proportion of iron oxide (as yellow ochre) with the manganese gives this pot a gingery under-painting. The dark ribs were painted on later, after the white slip coat.

Pot, 22 cm high, *c*. 1952. *Lucie Rie*.

Vase, 18 cm high, repaired, *c*. 1953. *Lucie Rie*.

Bottle, 32 cm high, 1957. *W. Ismay.*

Sgraffito self-portrait on canvas, and dated 1949,
24 × 18 cm. In foreground, pot with black mark
repeated on the opposite side. Height 16 cm, c. 1956.

Right: pot with geo-
metrical design, height
36 cm, c. 1952.

Poppy-head pot, 13 cm high, 1956, *W. Ismay*.

Deep bowl, 14 cm wide, *c.* 1955, with sgraffito design. The outside has white slip on manganese. The sgraffito design is cut through a thick coat of manganese and the inside of the bowl is then covered with a shiny white Lucie Rie glaze, which has an oily texture where it combines with the manganese, and an orange-peel surface where it is on its own.

Large bowl, 36 cm diameter, *c.* 1955, with a characteristic profile. The design inside shows a flying bird. The technique is the same as the bowl on the left, though both manganese and glaze coats are thinner.

Bowl with bird design, *c.* 1955, 42 cm diameter.
Unusually, this bowl has an ogee profile.

Left: large pot, 38 cm diameter. Sgraffito design through manganese, burnished. This pot was exhibited in Gothenburg in 1956.
Right: pot, 8 cm high. This beautiful tiny pot, made about 1953,
combines the surface and forms of Hans Coper's pots from the beginning of his career to the 1970s. *Jupp Dernbach*.

Pot with vertical groove impressed on one side.
Height: 13 cm, late 1950s. *Henry Rothschild*.

Two shapes with white glaze both inside and outside. Upper: 9 cms high, *Pat and Alan Firth*. Lower 11 cms high, *Francesca Coper*.

Left: bowl with semi-abstract design. Manganese and white glaze, 14 cm diameter. Hans painted an eye on all early bowls.

97

Pots made for the one-man show at Primavera in 1958. Many of the shapes presage pots of later date. The pot in the foreground on the left belongs to Lucie Rie. Sizes from 18–32 cm, all 1958.

Above: Four examples of 'tripots' made and photographed at Albion Mews, *c*. 1956. Average height: 20 cm.

Left: three bottle forms, surrounded by tableware on the shelves at the Albion Mews pottery, *c*. 1957. For the first half of his career Hans made many variations of this 'favourite shape', from 10 to 70 cm high (see pages 108–9). The early pots have barrel-shaped bodies, the later pots are more slender.

Spherical pot, 32 cm diameter. The purply-grey vitreous slip is perfect over every inch of this pot. Though it was made as early as 1956, when it was a present for Jane Gate, Hans never bettered it in terms of harmony between form and surface. *Jane Coper.*

Vase with incised lines filled with white slip, *c.* 1956, 29 cm high.

Three bottle forms made in 1958, 45–50 cm high, exhibited in Ceramics International 1959, Syracuse, USA.

Left and opposite: massive pots, *c.* 1958. The black pot far left, with radiating white stripes was described by *Architectural Review* as 'designed to hold flowers in large halls, staircases and churches.' It is 36 cm high. Next to it and shown in profile left is a large bottle form exhibited in the international exhibition at the Metropolitan Museum of Art in New York where it was described as 'England's only entry with claim to sculptural interest.' This big pot was an early example of a recurring form which became slimmer and lighter over the next two decades. See pages 118, 142 and 160.

Disc-form pot, 50 cm diameter, *c.* 1958. One of several similar forms made by joining two huge bowls rim to rim, decorated with scratches like sparks from a catherine wheel.

Left: pots on the kiln at Albion Mews awaiting firing. The pots on these pages illustrate Hans's preoccupation with a vertical form threading through a discus-form which is sometimes set on edge. The massive pot below right was exhibited in the English Potters 1960 exhibition in Rotterdam and was marked on the base 14 VII 60. 59 cm high.

Right: bottle form exhibited at the Boymans exhibition in 1967. Note the seal on the side of the pot. 16 cm high. Far right: large bottle and other pots awaiting finishing in the Digswell studio, c. 1960. Some of the heavy pots imprinted their own bases with the pattern of the wire mesh on which they were dried – a sure sign of a pot's having been made at Digswell. On the sculptor's stand is a massive flower vase nearly 60 cm high.

Typical pots from Digswell.

Black pots from the Digswell studio. Far left: 13 cm high, *Jupp Dernbach*; left: 22 cm high, *Lucie Rie*. Above left: scarcely visible in this photograph is the rectilinear incised collar on the front face of the pot, 28 cm high, *Ralph Brown*; centre: 30 cm high, *Boymans Museum*; right: *c.* 36 cm, whereabouts unknown. Right: hard-edged pot with well burnished surface. Height: 18 cm, *c.* 1964. *John Pike*.

Five brown-coloured Digswell pots photographed in the front studio at Digswell. Especially interesting is the distant pot on the left – a shape of which there is no other record.

Two-sided mural erected in 1962 at Swinton Comprehensive School, Yorkshire. The deep-relief discs in brown and cream vary from 30 cm to 60 cm in diameter, and are matched by similar discs on the other side of the wall. The wall surface around the discs is painted cream on both sides. In the first few years, pupils sent darts (paper ones) flying through the discs, but now there are perspex windows in the 'eyes', which also cuts down the draught.

The thistle shape first seen on page 106 is shown in more slender and elegant form in this small example, given to Lucie Rie in 1962. Note the concave profile at the top. Height: 24 cm. *Lucie Rie*.

Hans made very few examples of this form, though an inverted version of the shape can be seen on page 123. The pot shown here was always kept close to the artist in his workshop. Height including plinth: 17 cm, 1961. Unsigned.

Thistle form, *c.* 1962, height 28 cm. *Mr and Mrs J. Thompson.*

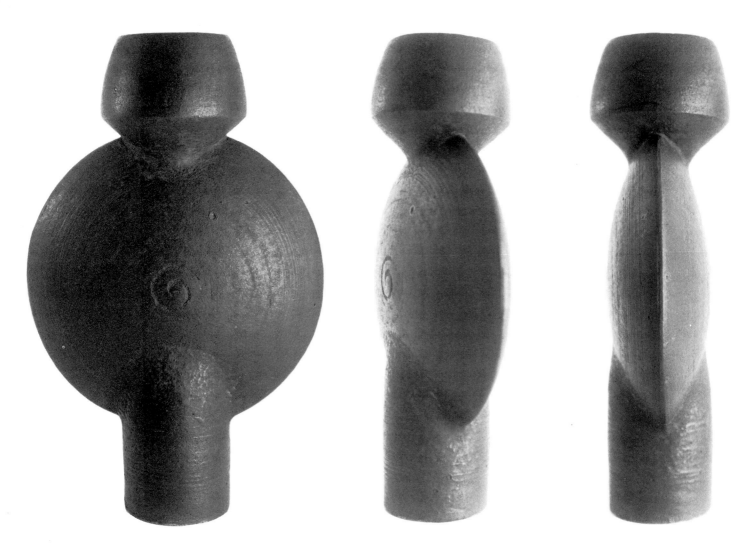

Three faces of a black pot typical of the Digswell period. The four thrown elements can most clearly be seen in the side view, right. Height: *c.* 24 cm, *c.* 1962. See also page 160.

The best of the tripots, 19 cm high, *c.* 1958. *Jane Coper.*

The very first of the hour-glass or onion shapes was made at Digswell. The pot is brown and cream in colour, 28 cm high. *Lucie Rie.*

Left: three hour-glass pots made in London in 1963, *c*. 29 cm high. See also title page.

Unusually wide examples of a vase shape much favoured by the artist in the early 1960s. Most of these small, hard-edged forms are black. The ones shown above are brown and cream, with horizontal incised lines made with a turning tool. Height: *c*. 9 cm, *c*. 1963.

The pot above was made in two pieces, and joined. Other examples of the shape, however, were left as two interlocking forms which could be separated and used independently as flower vases, each shape more elegant on its own than in the combination. The artist only made a few such pots in the early 1960s, *c.* 24 cm high.

Black pot from *c.* 1965 bears the spiral incised line much used on later work. Height: 13 cm.

Three versions of a form made only in the Hammersmith period. There was much variation in size, and in particular in the depth of the collar. Left: 37 cm high, above: 19 cm high, right: 18 cm high; all 1964–65.

The hour-glass pots became taller and more slender in the decade from 1965, but at the beginning of this period there were two distinct and short-lived developments, illustrated above. In the centre is the shape called 'dog bone' by Lucie Rie, with an emergent ring high up the collar – which links the shape with the very different pots on page 122–3. On the right is the wide-mouthed shape made in 1965. All these pots are relatively small – average height 19 cm.

Like Saturn with its rings, this tiny but beautifully finished pot shows the final development of the form on page 95. Diameter: 15·5 cm, 1966. *J. W. N. van Achterburgh.*

Left: tall bottles, *c.* 1967. The larger pot, *c.* 40 cm high, has the spiral incised line typical of later work. Right: bell shape with ring. Height: 24 cm, 1966. *Sainsbury Centre for Visual Arts.*

Throwing lines on the top section of the larger thistle shape above
indicate the method of making. The wide mouth of this design
(which was made originally as a flower container) was formed by
squeezing a shallow bowl so that its circular plan became long
and pointed like a canoe. The top was then trimmed level. The
pot in the foreground shows clearly the effect of burnishing the
black manganese surface. Heights: 24 and 19 cm, c. 1965.

Right: the pot in the foreground has
a white disc, and in that respect may
be unique. Height: c. 13 cm, 1965.

The small black pot above, with thick disc, is one of the earliest of a shape developed and refined in the 1960s, and illustrated in various forms below and on pages 132, 133 and 138–40. Height: 11 cm. Right: a classic example of the bulbous form on a stem. The final brushing of white slip to give a convex line on the form is a characteristic sign of pots from the mid 1960s. Height: 13 cm.

The central pot in the picture above shows the 'herringbone' pat-
terning of the surface which Hans Coper used about 1965. All the
pots above and right are 1963–65, and vary in height from 11 to
13 cm.

Late and delicate example of the hard-edged form made in the 1960 s also shown on page 121. Height : 9 cm. *Sainsbury Centre for Visual Arts.*

The pot in the centre, above, has an unusually wide disc top, with a thick vitrified glaze on the horizontal surface. Height: 20 cm, 1965. *W. Ismay.* The pot below has a thick coating of slip and is 35 cm high, 1965. *Boymans Museum.*

Right: bottle with deep texture, *c.* 25 cm high, *c.* 1965. Below: discs on the top of various bottle and bulbous forms of the 1960s.

This black pot was given to Lucie Rie in 1962. A very similar pot was bought by Bernard Leach the same year. Height: 20 cm. Right: white pot. The thick white slip has horizontal cracks which are deep but stable. Height: 20 cm, 1966.

Above: 14 cm high, 1970.
Sainsbury Centre for Visual Arts.

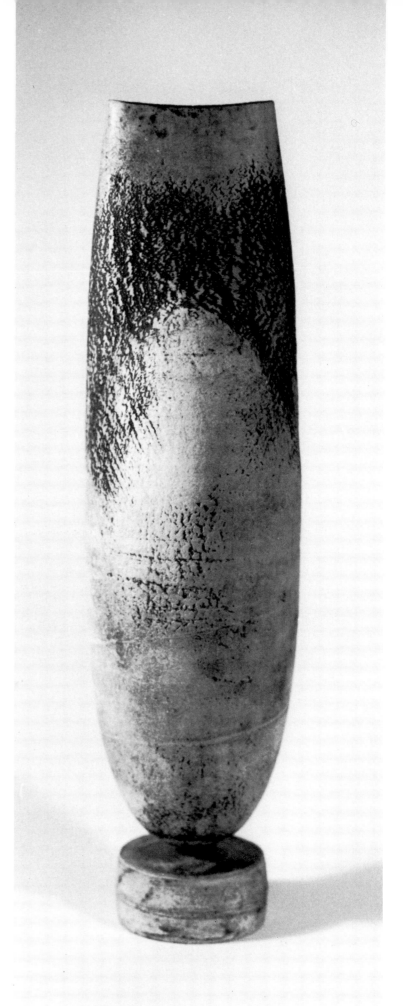

Right: presaging later forms and the first pot with a separately thrown base to be illustrated in this book, this pot from 1963 is unusual in its size – it is 37 cm high – and in the elongated oval of the main form. *D. and F. Kuyken-Schneider*. Far right: a delicate cup form with disc stands in front of a spherical form in the Hammersmith studio. Height: *c.* 15 cm, 1965.

Left: cup form, 1970, 13 cm high. *Sainsbury Centre for Visual Arts*. Right: composite form. The bowls which make up the central disc form were banded with manganese over a yellow ochre underpainting before assembly, and both manganese (dark brown) and ochre (ginger) show where the white slip has blistered. Height: 34 cm, 1970. *Sainsbury Centre for Visual Arts*.

Overleaf: a family of similar forms prepared for the Boymans Museum exhibition with Lucie Rie in 1967. Two new forms for the same exhibition make their first appearance in this book on page 143 – cup shape with vertical groove, in the foreground, and behind it the massive spade shape developed from 1966 onwards.

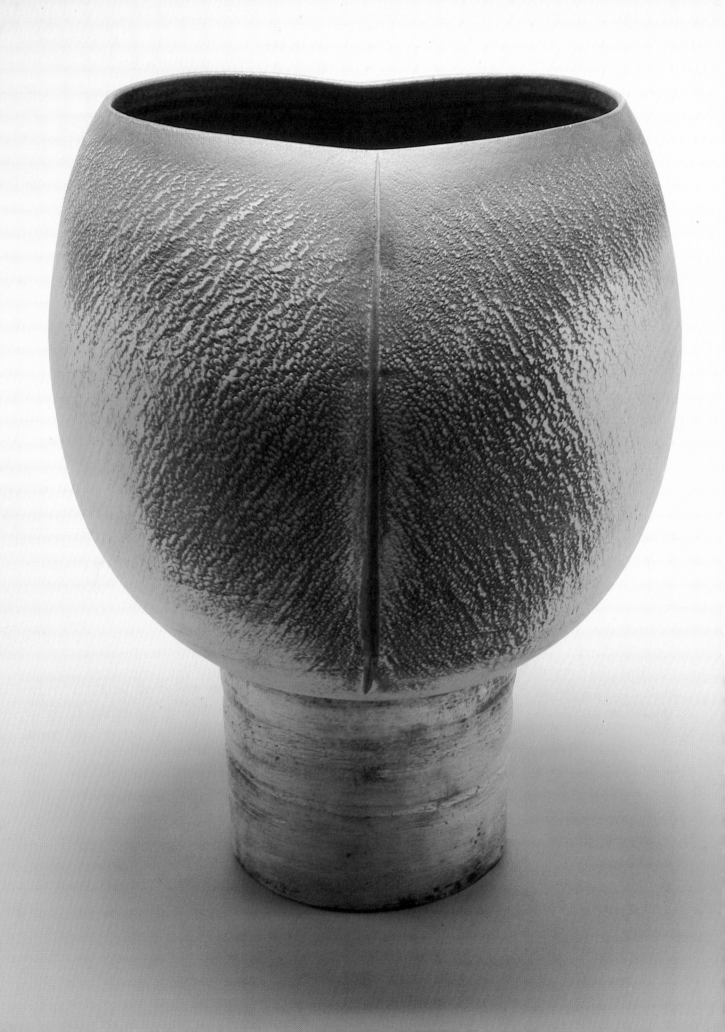

Hans Coper started making pots of the type shown here in 1966, and on page 143 is shown an early example which in terms of colour and tone is almost the negative of the pot illustrated on the right, height *c*. 15 cm, made about the same time. In the later pots the groove was carried to the rim, and the rim is distorted to a figure of eight. The majestic pot on the left was made about 1970. Height: 42 cm. *Clifford Sandelson*.

Pots from 1967, ranging in height from 12 to 45 cm.

Large pots on display at the Boymans
Museum, 1967.

The combination of a massive spherical
shape with a flattened cylinder was
developed in 1966, and continued with
variations in the proportions of the two
parts for a decade. Behind the pot,
which is 42 cm high, is a photograph of
a Cycladic stone carving from the British
Museum which Hans kept in his studio.

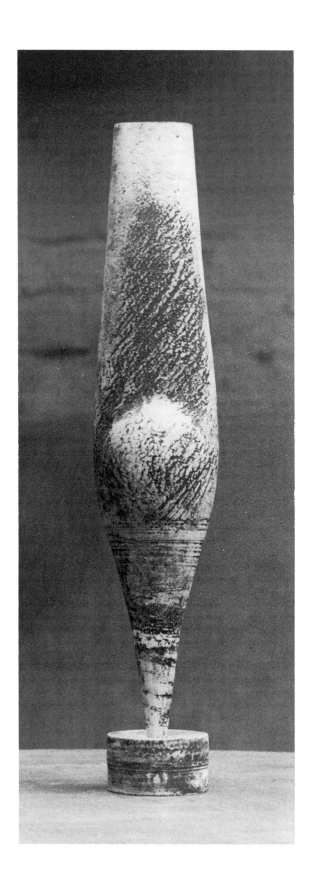

The pots shown left and above are essentially a combination of the same forms as on the previous two pages, though with an added base for stability. The shallow thrown drums on the two pots above were fixed to the forms by drilling both parts and cementing in a section of steel knitting needle. Heights: 20–28 cm, 1967.

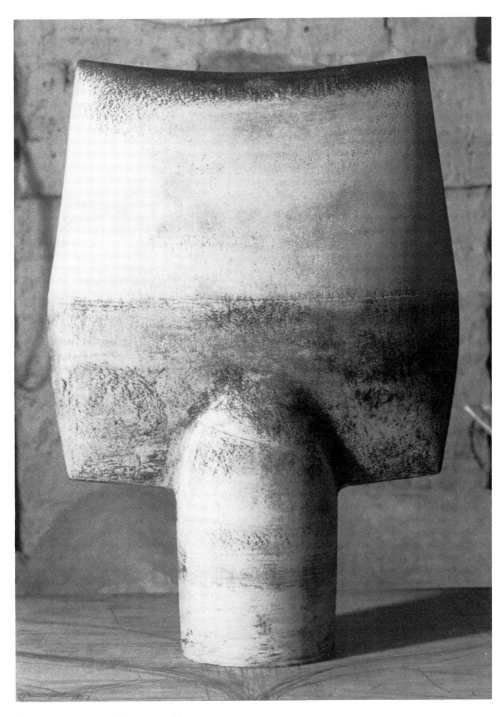

The spade shape made its first public appearance
in 1967 at the Boymans Museum. The photograph
above was taken for the catalogue. Height: 21 cm.

Four composite forms made in Hammersmith in 1967. Height: 26 cm.

This pot, like others of the same family, is made in
two pieces, and joined at the narrowest point. It has
a deep spiral groove. Height: 32 cm, 1970. *W. Ismay.*

Above and right: pots made in the new studio at Frome in 1968 in preparation for the exhibition at the Victoria & Albert Museum. The black pot above is a shape familiar since the Digswell years, but behind can be seen part of a completely new ovoid shape which Hans continued to make for the rest of his life.

154

Pots made for the Victoria & Albert Museum exhibition, 1969. Heights: 20–45 cm.

'Coper's pots have an austere look. . . . Their shapes suggest primitive forms out of which the first sculpture might have grown. It can be no accident that the words which most readily rise to mind to describe their shapes are figurative: shouldered, necked, beaked, cleft, waisted and so on. Their hollowness or flatness, fullness or slenderness . . . seems related, like all art that matters, to our experience of ourselves and of the world around us.' Edwin Mullins reviewing the Victoria & Albert exhibition in the *Sunday Telegraph*, February 1969.

Above: Hans's preoccupation with anthropomorphic forms continued through his career. The three small pots above were amongst the last he made. Heights: 21–25·5 cm, c. 1977. Centre pot, *Sainsbury Centre for Visual Arts.*

Left : side view of the pot shown on page 141. Right : massive thistle form, 45 cm high, 1972. *Doreen and Ted Appleby.*

The bottle forms of the sixties (pages 134–5) were subtly changed by the 1970s into the forms illustrated here – each with four symmetrical dents in the body accentuated by horizontal incised lines. Heights: 19–20 cm, all 1970–72. Far left: *Dr Ekkart Klinge*, left: *Harald Muhlhausen*. Above centre: *Sainsbury Centre for Visual Arts*. Left and right: *Henry Rothschild*.

A very rare form, *c.* 1969, 13·5 cm high. *J. W. N. van Achterbergh*.

163

Above: flattened form based on a cylinder. At the shoulder the sides are joined to make an edge like an axe blade. Height: 18·5 cm, 1970. *Lucie Rie*.

Right: squeezed form with four symmetrical dents. Inside the main form is another cylinder better to hold the stems of flowers. Height: 23 cm, 1970. *Muriel Rose*.

Above: squeezed form with four symmetrical dents, accentuated with manganese and deep texturing. Height: 23 cm, 1975. *Sainsbury Centre for Visual Arts*.

Above and left: two versions of a favourite shape. Most were rounded and white, as above (height: 20 cm, 1970). The sharper form left (height: 12·5 cm, 1974), burnished black, is rare. *D. and F. Kuyken-Schneider.*

The same techniques and components produce pots of different characters. Left: 1970, 15·5 cm high. Below: 1970, 15 cm high. *Sainsbury Centre for Visual Arts.*

Right: very large pot, 75 cm high, 30 cm wide, inscribed underneath: 1.X.1972 HC. To Writhlington School. Thank you for Jennea the goat. *Writhlington School.*

Spade shapes seen from front and side. Heights: 17–35 cm, c. 1972.

Five spade forms, 1970–72. Above: left and centre, 13·5 cm, *Jane Coper*; right, 14 cm, *Sainsbury Centre for Visual Arts*. Facing page: far right, 21 cm, right, 13·5 cm, both *Sainsbury Centre for Visual Arts*.

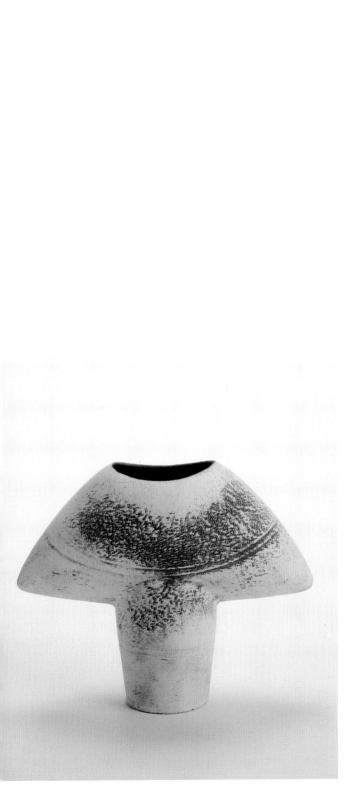

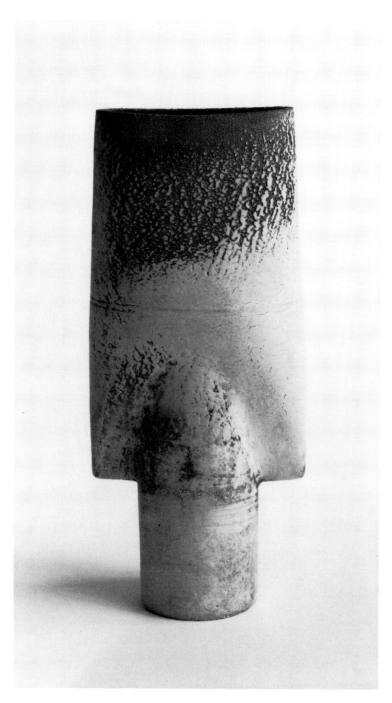

Spade form, 14 cm high, c. 1971.

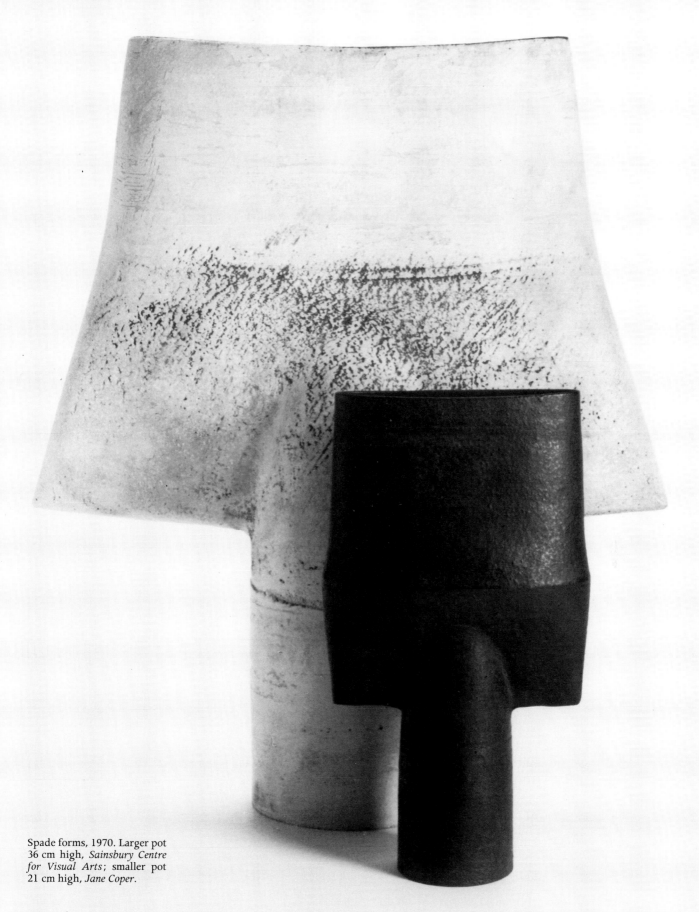

Spade forms, 1970. Larger pot
36 cm high, *Sainsbury Centre
for Visual Arts*; smaller pot
21 cm high, *Jane Coper*.

Thistle form. Height: 24 cm, 1972.
Sainsbury Centre for Visual Arts.

Left: metrication in 1971 changed the proportions of ingredients in Hans's white slip slightly, giving for a time a darker coloration to finished pots, as in the pot at left (22 cm high) in which the bulbous form sits in a drum-like base, like an egg in a cup. 1972. *Jane Coper.* The smaller pot (17 cm high) has symmetrical dents and a simple junction to its stem. 1972. *Max Meyer.*

Dark under-painting shows through blisters in the slip. Height: 18 cm, 1972. *Sainsbury Centre for Visual Arts.*

Standing form heavily coated with manganese and burnished. Height: 18 cm, 1969. *Henry Rothschild*.

Ovoid pot with vertical grooves. The most original and powerful form of Hans's last years. Height: 30 cm, 1975. *G. K. Zunz.*

All the pots on these pages were exhibited at the Robert Welch Gallery, Chipping Camden, in 1975. Some of the forms were completely new, including the egg-in-cup forms left, 13·5–20 cm high. Hans's own evaluation of the pots was clear from the differential in the prices asked, and the magnificent and unusual form above was one of the highest-priced. It was not sold.

White globular form, 24 cm high, *c*. 1975.
Sainsbury Centre for Visual Arts.

Right: a rare shape, exhibited at Chipping
Camden in 1975. Height: 17 cm. *G. Walker.*

The globular shape rising on a funnel-shaped stem from a cubic base was one of the last shapes made by Hans, and very few examples exist. Most were burnished black, and the grey-green glaze used for the base came from Lucie Rie. Height: both *c.* 21 cm, *c.* 1975.

Three late forms from 1975–76, 21–22 cm. Above and right: *Sainsbury Centre for Visual Arts*; left: *Jane Coper*.

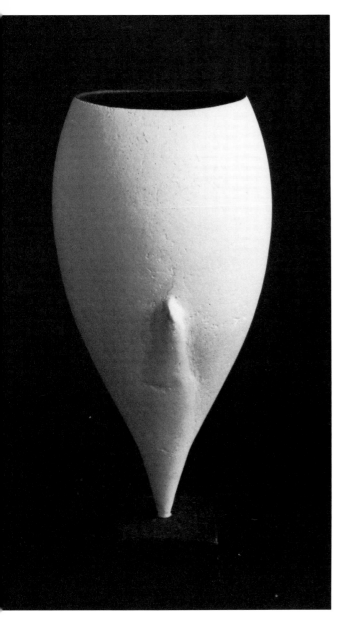

Above: white form supported by black base. Height:
28 cm, c. 1972. *Laurens Coper*.

One form slides into another, both in the literal sense
and in a less obvious way: one type viewed from the
side strongly echoes another from the 'front'. The
pots on the right are the same pots as those on the
left in the picture opposite. Height: 16–24 cm,
c. 1972.

White form, 31 cm high, 1975. The ring of bare clay on the main form was where the pot was supported in the kiln by a collar. *W. Ismay*. Right: squared-off form on drum base, with hollow impressions on two sides. The bluish cast to the slip on the pot occurred on pots made in 1975. Actual size.

The horizontal incised line accentuates the dents on these white pots of 1975. They represent the most refined versions of the finest later forms. Heights: left, 21 cm, right, 22·5 cm.

The pot above on its tall stem was the last pot completed by Hans Coper. Height: 17 cm, 1979.

Like a ripe plum, this small burnished pot is uniquely marked with a vertical groove. Height: 14 cm, *c.* 1975. *Ed. Wolf.*

Burnished cup form on a drum base. Height:
12 cm, 1974. *Sainsbury Centre for Visual Arts.*

An ochre colour penetrates the white slip on this standing form. Height: 21 cm, 1975. *Pat and Alan Firth*.

An array of Cycladic forms. The photographs left and far right show pots exhibited in Chipping Camden in 1975. The black pot centre right is almost unique: of this late shape made after 1975 only four were burnished black. Height: 28 cm. *Sainsbury Centre for Visual Arts.*

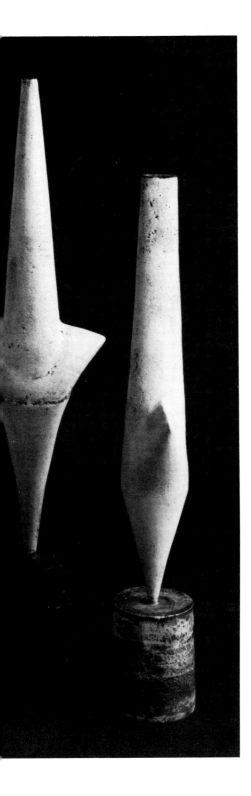

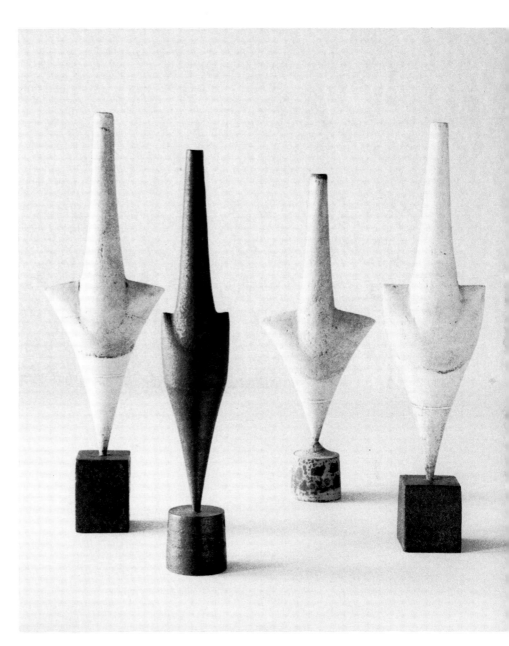

Left: Cycladic forms from the front and in profile, 23–30 cm high, 1975. Above: pots from the Chipping Camden exhibition, 1975, 25–32 cm high. Left pot: *Graeme James*; centre left, *Dr Rollo Ballantyne*, centre right, *Sainsbury Centre for Visual Arts*; right, *Harley Carpenter*.

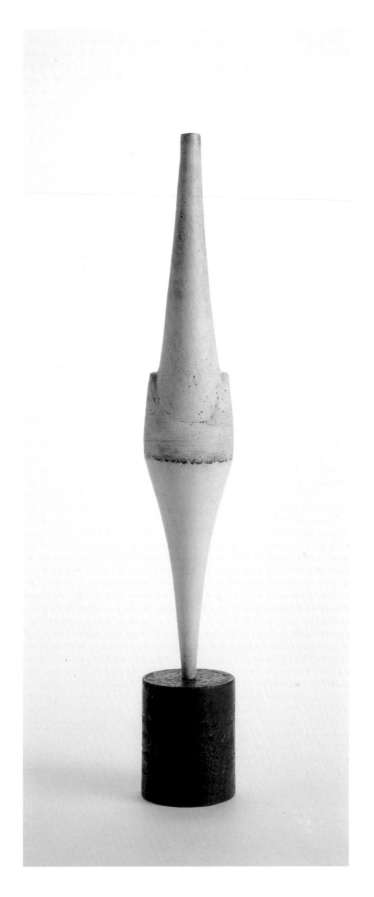

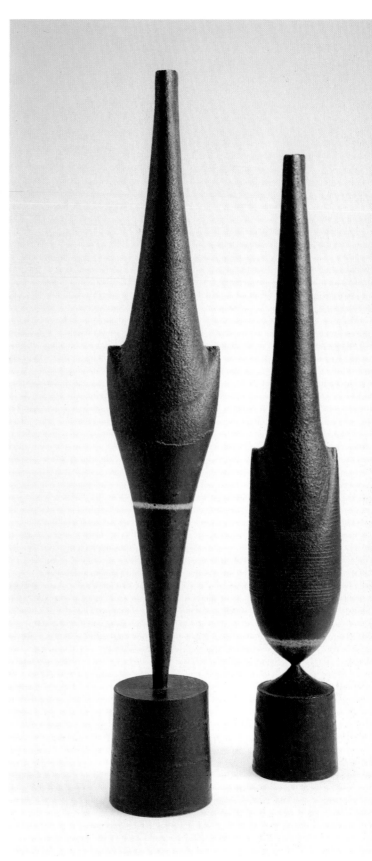

Cycladic forms, 1974–76, 28– 32 cm high.
All: *Sainsbury Centre for Visual Arts.*

Left : burnished black pot, squared-off top, with impressions on both sides. The hard turning line below the impression was a characteristic of late pots. Height : 13·5 cm, *c.* 1975. *Tony Birks.* Right : Four of the five white pots made in this shape, standing on the wheelhead in the Frome studio. The fifth pot in the series is shown on page 196, left. Height : 29·31 cm, 1976.

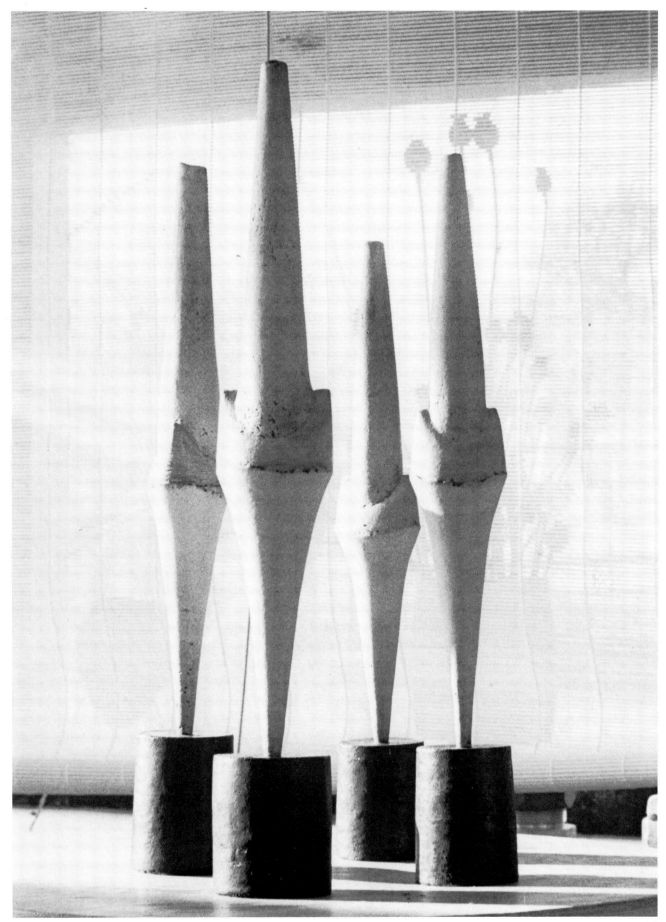

Black burnished pot with incised decoration. Height: 14 cm, 1973. *Henry Rothschild*.

Composite forms with thick white slip. Left:
24 cm high, *c*. 1972, *David Holt*; right: 19·5 cm
high, 1972. *Sainsbury Centre for Visual Arts*.

'A predynastic Egyptian pot, roughly egg-shaped, the size of my hand: made thousands of years ago it has survived in more than one sense. A humble, passive, somehow absurd object — yet potent, mysterious, sensuous. It conveys no comment, no self-expression, but seems to contain and reflect its maker and the human world it inhabits, to contribute its minute quantum of energy.' *Hans Coper, 1969*

Ovoid pot, 24·5 cm high, 1975.
Sainsbury Centre for Visual Arts.

Technical Notes

The focus of Hans Coper's work was on form, and the perfection of two contrasting surfaces, one light, one black, and so the spectrum of clays, glazes and firing methods is a great deal narrower than that of most potters. It is for this reason that the colour and surface of the pots in the illustration section of this book are not described in detail individually, as they are all basically the same. For those interested, however, the following technical notes have been prepared, with the help of David Queensberry.

Clays

Apart from very early works and tableware made jointly with Lucie Rie, Hans used only two clay bodies, a white clay for his light pots and a coloured clay for the black pots, this second body being basically a modification of the white clay. The white clay is 'T' material, which is a ball clay containing a coarse white fireclay grog. It used to be manufactured at Pontypridd in South Wales, but is currently available from Morgan Refractories at Neston in the Wirral, Cheshire.

In order to make the coloured clay for his black pots Hans modified the 'T' material according to the following formula:

'T' material	73·2%
Red clay	18·3%
Manganese dioxide	1·2%
China clay	7·3%

When uncoated with colourant, this clay fires a greyish red-brown, speckled with white grog.

Slips and Colourants

Hans's white slip was made from feldspar whiting and china clay, in proportions which the artist never revealed. Slip is essentially a precipitate of solids in water, and usually has a consistency, when applied, of thin cream. Hans added a little gum arabic in the proportion of one teaspoon to about 500cc of slip, to help adhesion to the dry pot. Slip is usually applied to an unfired pot when it is leather-hard, but Hans always painted slip on to the outside surface of a bone-dry pot. Gum arabic was for this reason all the more important, to prevent the slip from flaking off. He used a variety of brushes, from soft-haired, mop-headed brushes to house painters' brushes, mostly the latter.

For the black pots a mixture of manganese dioxide and iron oxide in the form of yellow ochre, in the approximate proportions of 3:2, was used, mixed with water and gum arabic.

The interior of pots was darkened with the above mixture by pouring the liquid into the pot from a jug, swilling around, and pouring out the surplus.

Firing

All the ware was fired to 1250°C in an electric kiln, using Seger cone 8 as a temperature guide. Hans's kiln records show how carefully he watched the rise in temperature of the kiln, which has to be very slow in the early stages for once-fired ware because of the chemically-combined water in the clay molecule.

The black pots required a maturing temperature some ten degrees lower than the white pots, and for this reason were always stacked in the bottom of the kiln, which in the case of electric kilns is slightly cooler than elsewhere in the chamber.

The atmosphere in an electric kiln is oxidising. The oxygen-starved or 'reducing' atmosphere achievable in a combustible fuel kiln – wood, oil, gas, etc. – would have produced an effect on the colour of his pots, especially the white ones, though I do not know if he ever experimented with reduction.

Finishing

Hans used a metal scouring pad called 'Springo' to scratch the surface of unfired pots, and possibly also to burnish the exteriors after firing. Certainly Hans paid a great deal of attention to the pot after it had left the kiln, not only sealing the interior with furniture wax to ensure that it was waterproof ('T' material is a notoriously 'open' clay, even at stoneware temperatures), but also using an emery disc attached to an electric drill as a burnisher. This disc would burnish convex surfaces, but not concave ones, and perhaps the 'Springo' was used for these.

There is a very marked difference between the unburnished surface, which is dry, and the burnished surface, which has a graphite-like sheen. Hans managed to get his burnishing tool into the crannies of even very small pots.

Definitions

'Engobe' is a word sometimes used to describe semi-vitrified dry looking surfaces, halfway between a glaze and a slip. Major ingredients in the materials Hans used on the surface – feldspar in the white slip and manganese dioxide in the black – will vitrify all by themselves at the right temperatures to produce a vitreous surface. Some would argue that Hans's pots were glazed, and others that the surface was an engobe. I would prefer to call the surface a slip, but it really does not matter.

Hans Coper's seals were made in plaster of Paris or low-fired fine red clay, and varied in size from 1 cm to over 3 cm in diameter. He intended them to be seen as shown below, like a bowl on a wheel, rather than as the initials HC. Occasionally they were placed on the side of the pot, as in the example top right. The rare 'square' seal bottom left was used only occasionally, and only on pots made at Frome. Other designs exist.

Unfortunately, photographs of the seals are subject to the 'reversing effect' – try to see the seals in each instance as impressions pushed into the pot, rather than as bumps standing out in relief. The seals below are all shown $1\frac{1}{2}$ × actual size.

Acknowledgements

To prepare a book about the work and life of Hans Coper would have been impossible without the help and cooperation of Jane Coper and Lucie Rie, and I am immensely grateful to them both. All other friends and colleagues of Hans mentioned in the text and a great many more besides, have without exception been keen to offer their help in recalling experiences and facts, which is an eloquent tribute in itself to Hans.

For their confidence and material support I am indebted to Sir Robert and Lady Sainsbury, who said, when surrounded by examples of thirty years of Hans's work, 'There must be a book.'

T.B.

March 1983

Chronology

1920	April 8: Hans Coper born in Chemnitz, Lower Saxony, now Karlmarxstadt in German Democratic Republic.
1933	Coper family moves from Reichenbach to Dresden.
1935	Family moves to Leipzig.
1936	June: suicide of Julius Coper. Mrs Coper and two sons return to Dresden.
1937	Walter Coper leaves Germany for Argentina.
1939	Hans Coper leaves Germany for England.
1940	May: Hans is arrested in London and interned as enemy alien. July: sent to Canada.
1941	June: returns to England. July: enrols in Pioneer Corps.
1943	April: discharged from Army. October: marries Annie Penelope Karaiskos.
1944	March: daughter Ingrid born. Hans and Francesca move to Camden Town. December: daughter Anya born.
1946	Meets Lucie Rie and begins work at Albion Mews Pottery.
1948	November: son Laurens born.
1950	November: shares exhibition, at Berkeley Galleries, London, with Lucie Rie.
1951	April–October: Festival of Britain.
1952	March: marriage with Penelope Coper dissolved. July: International Conference of Craftsmen in Pottery and Textiles, Dartington Hall, Devon.
1953	Contributes to English Potters Exhibition, Stedelijk Museum, Amsterdam.
1954	Gold Medal winner at Milan Triennale. Shares exhibition with Lucie Rie at Berkeley Galleries. Meets Jane Gate in London.
1955	Shares exhibition with Lucie Rie at Röhsska Konstslöjdmuseet, Gothenburg.
1956	One-man show at Bonniers, New York. Shares exhibition with Lucie Rie at Berkeley Galleries.
1957	Shares exhibition with Lucie Rie at University of Minnesota, Minneapolis.
1958	January: becomes naturalised British subject. May: first one-man show in England, at Primavera, Sloane Street, London.
1959	January: moves to Digswell, Hertfordshire. Contributor to Ceramics International, Syracuse, USA. Contributor to Smithsonian Institution travelling exhibition, British Artist Craftsmen. One of founder members of architectural group at Digswell.
1960	Contributor to Boymans Museum English Potters exhibition, Rotterdam. Contributor to Midland Group exhibition, Nottingham.

Walter Coper visits Hans in England.
1961 Starts teaching at Camberwell School of Art.
1962 Coventry Cathedral candlesticks installed.
1963 Moves from Digswell to Princedale Road, London.
1964 Contributor to Ceramics International, Tokyo.
      Moves workshop to studio off Upper Mall,
      Hammersmith.
1965 October: one-man show at Berkeley Galleries.
      December: contributor to The Potter's World
      exhibition at the Molton Gallery, London.
1966 September: starts teaching at the Royal College of
      Art.
1967 April: joint exhibition with Lucie Rie at Boymans
      Museum, Rotterdam. Hans travels to Holland for
      opening.
      June: Boymans exhibition moves to Gemeente
      Museum, Arnhem.
      August: Hans and Jane move to Spring Gardens,
      Frome.
1968 Contributor to mixed exhibition British Potters at
      Qantas Gallery, London.
1969 January: joint exhibition with Peter Collingwood at
      Victoria & Albert Museum, London.
      March: featured in Van Achterbergh Collection
      exhibition in Boymans Museum, Rotterdam.
1970 Contributor to Smithsonian Institution travelling
      exhibition, British Designer Craftsmen.
      Exhibits in British Pavilion, Expo 70, Osaka;
      Takashimaya exhibition, Tokyo and National
      Museum of Modern Art, Kyoto.
      Contributor to Den Permanente Exhibition,
      Copenhagen.
      One man show at Midland Group gallery,
      Nottingham.
1971 Contributor to exhibition at City Art Gallery,
      Bradford, Yorkshire.
      Contributor to Kettle's Yard exhibition, Cambridge
      (also 1972, 1974, 1975).
1972 Joint exhibition with Lucie Rie at Museum für
      Kunst und Gewerbe, Hamburg.
      Contributor to International Ceramics exhibition,
      Victoria & Albert Museum, London.
1974 December: marries Jane Gate.
1975 Last British exhibition, at Robert Welch Gallery,
      Chipping Camden, Glos.
      Amyotrophic lateral sclerosis diagnosed.
1980 April: sixtieth birthday exhibition, Hetjens
      Museum, Dusseldorf.
1981 June 16: Hans dies at Frome.
1983 January: opening of Memorial Collection at
      Sainsbury Centre for the Visual Arts, University of
      East Anglia, Norwich.
      September: Hans Coper exhibition at Sainsbury
      Centre.

1984 January–March: Hans Coper exhibition, Hetjens
      Museum, Dusseldorf.
      March–May: Hans Coper exhibition, Boymans
      Museum, Rotterdam.
      June–July: Hans Coper exhibition, Serpentine
      Gallery, London

Some of the public collections containing Hans Coper's pots
are as follows: Amsterdam: Stedelijk Museum; Arnhem:
Gemeente Museum; Bath: Holbourne of Menstrie Museum;
Bradford: City Art Gallery and Museum; Cardiff: National
Museum of Wales; Detroit: Institute of Arts; Dusseldorf:
Hetjens Museum; Gothenburg: Röhsska Konstslöjdmuseet;
Hamburg: Museum für Kunst und Gewerbe; Kyoto:
National Museum of Modern Art; Leeds: Temple Newsam
House; London: Victoria & Albert Museum; New York:
Museum of Modern Art; Oslo: Nordenfjeldske
Kunstindustrimuseum; Rotterdam: Museum Boymans van
Beuningen; s'Hertogenbosch: Kruithuis; Zurich:
Kunstgewerbe Museum; public collections in Bristol,
Leicester, Melbourne, Stockholm, Toronto and Wakefield.

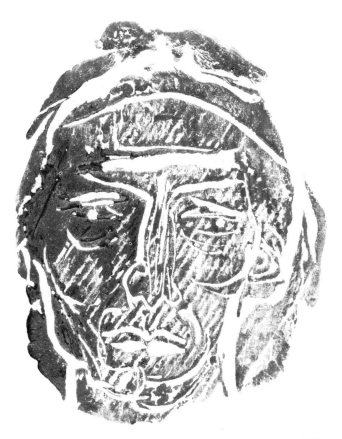

Bibliography

Birks, Tony, *Art of the Modern Potter*. London & New York 1967, revised 1976, 1982

Casson, Michael, *Potters in Britain Today*. London 1967

Charleston, R. J., *World Ceramics*. London 1968

Digby, George Wingfield, *The Work of the Modern Potter*. 1951

Houston, John (Ed.), *Lucie Rie*. London 1981

Lane, Peter, *Studio Ceramics*. London 1983

Lewenstein, Eileen and Emmanuel Cooper, *New Ceramics*. London & New York 1974

Lucie-Smith, Edward, *World of the Makers*. London & New York 1975

Rose, Muriel, *Artist Potters in England*. London 1955, revised 1970

Magazine articles, catalogues and pamphlets

Ceramic Review, London, Nos. 5, 7, 11, 17, 21, 25, 33, 36, 62, 66, 71, 73, 76, 77, 78

Collingwood/Coper: A Picture Book 1969. Victoria & Albert Museum, London 1969

Hans Coper (pamphlet). Hetjens Museum, Dusseldorf 1980

Crafts Magazine, London, No. 52, 1981; No. 54, 1982

The Craftsman's Art (catalogue), Victoria & Albert Museum, London 1972

Design Magazine, London, No. 247, 1969

International Ceramics (catalogue), Victoria & Albert Museum, London 1972

Kunst + Handwerk. Dusseldorf 1980

The Metropolitan Museum of Art Bulletin. New York February 1959

Lucie Rie and Hans Coper (catalogue). Boymans Museum, Rotterdam 1967

Lucie Rie and Hans Coper (catalogue). Museum für Kunst und Gewerbe, Hamburg 1972

The Saturday Book. London 1969/1970

Picture Credits

All the photographs in this book have been taken by Jane Coper, with the exception of the following: Alphabet and Image: pages: 127 (lower), 138 (right), 163 (lower), 166 (lower); H. Boehm: 20, 21 (bottom); H. Carpenter: 68; Angela Coombes: 65; Francesca Coper: 26; Angela Demmer: 30; Euan Duff: 71, 108 (lower), 153, 167, 170, 180–1 (all), 194 (left), 195 (right); Fox Photos: 13; Carole Houston: 112 (lower), 113 (lower); Edgar Hyman: 67; William Ismay: 51 (both); Landesbildstelle Rheinland: 162 (top); Genia Leviné: 69; Maillard Studio: 45; Harald Muhlhausen: 162 (lower); Arthur Ross: 15 (both); Robert Welch: 72; Hugh White Studios (photo Dennis Smith): 82 (top), 83; Dick Wolters: 62–3, 149; Adrian Wood: 48 (top). The photographers of the following are unknown: pages 9, 10 (both), 14, 19, 21 (top), 24 (both), 28 (both), 53, 70. Book design by the author with Albert Clamp.